W9-BCY-022

4-57

THE REPRESENTATIVE:
TRUSTEE? DELEGATE? PARTISAN? POLITICO?

PROBLEMS IN POLITICAL SCIENCE
under the editorial direction of NEAL RIEMER, *University of Wisconsin-Milwaukee*

WESTERN EUROPE: WHAT PATH TO INTEGRATION?
edited by CAROL EDLER BAUMANN, *University of Wisconsin-Milwaukee*

THE REPRESENTATIVE: TRUSTEE? DELEGATE? PARTISAN? POLITICO?
edited by NEAL RIEMER, *University of Wisconsin-Milwaukee*

FREE SPEECH AND POLITICAL PROTEST
edited by MARVIN SUMMERS, *University of Wisconsin-Milwaukee*

OTHER VOLUMES IN PREPARATION

PROBLEMS IN POLITICAL SCIENCE

The Representative:

TRUSTEE? DELEGATE? PARTISAN? POLITICO?

EDITED WITH AN INTRODUCTION BY
Neal Riemer
University of Wisconsin-Milwaukee

D. C. HEATH AND COMPANY BOSTON

FOR DAVID RAPHAEL RIEMER

320.082
H437
v.2

Library of Congress Catalog Card Number: 67–27818

COPYRIGHT © 1967 BY D. C. HEATH AND COMPANY

No part of the material covered by this copyright
may be reproduced in any form without written
permission of the publisher. Printed in the
United States of America

Printed July 1967

Table of Contents

Introduction

I. Styles of Representation

II. The Representative in Perspective

58639

The Clash of Ideas

THE REPRESENTATIVE AS TRUSTEE

[W]e must place first the responsibility we owe not to our party or even to our constituents but to our individual consciences.

—JOHN F. KENNEDY

It is likely, therefore, that the representative has become less and less a delegate and more and more a trustee as the business of government has become more and more intricate and technical as well as less locally centered.

—JOHN WAHLKE, HEINZ EULAU, WILLIAM BUCHANAN, AND LeROY F. FERGUSON

THE REPRESENTATIVE AS DELEGATE

The representative, therefore, must in the nature of things, represent his particular constituents only . . . must express the will, and speak the opinions, of the constituents that depute him.

—ACTS OF THE COMMONWEALTH OF VIRGINIA, 1812

If the Congressman were a modern Machiavelli, his advice to freshmen in Congress on "How to Stay in Office" would be: (1) Vote for the home folks first, especially for those who are well organized; (2) keep on good terms with the local party bosses; (3) stress your protection of your district's interests as a whole against the outside world; (4) as far as possible do not commit yourself on the important national issues that divide your constituents.

—JAMES M. BURNS

THE REPRESENTATIVE AS PARTISAN

Once the basic test policies of the majority party have been selected, the congressmen of that party would be required to vote with the party on bills designed to put these policies into action.

—HENRY WALLACE

Quantitative analysis of roll call votes shows, contrary to majority opinion, that significant differences exist between our major parties. . . . Party pressure seems to be more effective than any other pressure on congressional voting. . . .

—JULIUS TURNER

THE REPRESENTATIVE AS POLITICO

Whether legislators say they are Trustees voting on the merits of bills, Delegates voting in accordance with demands of districts or interest groups, or Partisans voting in accordance with preconceived positions of their political party, they are actually all Politicos, who vote on different bases depending on the issues confronting them.

—WILDER CRANE

The average legislator appears, then, to make no firm commitment to constituency, party, or self. Their demands on him and their sanctions over him shift from issue to issue. Both the shifting political demands and the finely balanced equities of choice force him to choose only tentatively and cautiously, one issue at a time.

—FRANK J. SORAUF

Introduction

Styles of Representation

The central problem of this volume can be phrased as follows: *How do we understand the role of the representative?* The more strictly ethical selections included herein speak to this question: Should the representative be a Trustee? A Delegate? A Partisan? A Politico? These four "ideal-types," or models, may initially provide us with a convenient, if oversimplified, way of understanding the modern role of the representative.

Should the representative, as a Trustee, follow his own conscience, his own judgment of what is in the best interest of his nation or of his political constituency? Should he, as a Trustee, rely upon his superior knowledge of complicated legislative problems, and rise above the selfish and narrow interests of his constituents, petty partisan pressures, and legislative "wheeling and dealing?" Should he, as a Trustee of the welfare of his people and the Nation, lead his constituents and the Nation in attaining their best long-range interests?

Or should the representative, as a Delegate (or Agent), dutifully vote as his constituents, or at least a majority of them, would vote if they were, themselves, consulted? Should he as a democratic Delegate, suppress his private prejudices, ignore the dictates of party, the pleas of special interests outside his constituency, the arguments of his legislative colleagues, and express, as best he can, the wishes of the people who elected him? Will the public interest best emerge from the honest expression of the will of the people as voiced by their faithful agents?

Or should the representative, as a Partisan, adhere responsibly to the party platform upon which he was elected and which the majority who voted for him expect him to fulfill? Should he, as a responsible member of a political party, resist his own personal ideas of national welfare, the clamour of well-heeled interests, even the momentary fury of constituents, and vote for a legislative program which the electorate has approved by returning a

1

majority of his party to office in a democratic election? Should he, as a loyal party member, stick with the party caucus's interpretation of key legislative issues?

Or should the representative, as a Politico, attempt to combine the roles of Trustee, Delegate, and Partisan, and thus follow his conscience on some issues, his constituents on others, and the party on still others? Should he, as a Politico, and depending on the circumstances, balance conscience, constituency, and party in order to do justice, respectively, to his (1) own sense of what is best for the nation or constituency, (2) understanding of democratic service or need for reelection, and (3) belief in party responsibility or recognition of party power?

These models or "ideal-types," above, have been presented sympathetically. A hostile understanding of these four roles might be phrased as follows: Should the representative be a conceited, unresponsive, phony aristocrat (i.e., a Trustee)? A fearful, spineless lackey of the multitude (i.e., a Delegate)? A cowardly, party rubber-stamp (i.e., a Partisan)? Or a wishy-washy, cynical Machiavellian (i.e., a Politico)?

Other selections in this volume reveal a more empirical understanding of the role of the representative. How is his role perceived by the public or by representatives themselves? How is his role performed? Why does he behave as he does? The empirical answers to these questions may either support or attack a given ethical approach to the representative's role. The selections included here present studies of both state and national representatives. Because the findings are not always in agreement, the student will want to ask why they are not. Do roles shift from state to state? From the states to the nation? Why? Because of different conditions? Which? Were the studies made at different times? Were different research designs used? All these questions suggest the need to appraise the research done in this field with a critical eye.

The Representative as a Trustee

Edmund Burke, in his classic "Speech to the Electors of Bristol," still remains the most famous advocate of the *Trustee* model of representation. Burke conceded that the representative ought "to live in . . . the closest correspondence . . . with his constituents." "But," Burke continued, "his unbiased opinion, his mature judgment, his enlightened conscience, he ought not to sacrifice to . . .

any man." These were "a trust from Providence, for the abuse of which he is deeply answerable." For Burke, government and legislation were "matters of reason and judgment, and not of inclination. . . ." Discussion must precede determination. The will of the constituency could not automatically be related to the nation's issues. Hence *"authoritative* instructions, *mandates* issued, which a member is bound blindly and implicitly to obey, to vote, and to argue for, though contrary to the clearest conviction of his judgment and conscience," were mistaken!

In his Pulitzer Prize-winning book, *Profiles in Courage,* Senator John F. Kennedy illustrated this Burkean position in modern America. In his first chapter, Kennedy set the stage for his subsequent accounts of a number of brave Senators who bucked party and constituent pressures, and who risked their careers, to follow their consciences. He reached the conclusion that the "voters selected us . . . because they had confidence in our judgment and our ability to exercise that judgment from a position where we could determine what were their own best interests, as a part of the nation's interests."

John Wahlke, Heinz Eulau, and their colleagues in a 1959 study of four states—California, New Jersey, Ohio, and Tennessee— found that 63 percent of the states' legislators defined themselves as Trustees, 23 percent as Politicos, and 14 percent as Delegates. They concluded that rather "than being a 'pious formula,' the role orientation of trustee may be a functional necessity." Under modern conditions the trustee orientation is probably more realistic than the other roles perceived.

The Representative as a Delegate

The *Delegate* model, with its corollary of instructions against which Burke argued, is illustrated with an historical selection from Alfred de Grazia's stimulating book, *Public and Republic.* As the Virginia legislature, reflecting the influence of Rousseau, reasoned in 1812: to obtain a true general will based upon a true expression of individual wills, "the representative must express the will, and speak the opinions, of the constituents that depute him." In this fashion was the "Doctrine of Instructions," popular in the late 18th and 19th centuries, explained and justified.

In the 20th Century, Philosopher-Congressman T. V. Smith, has defended the Delegate theory. "It is indeed the primary business of Congress to discern and follow the popular will when there is a popular will, and to do nothing where there isn't, save to talk around and about until there is a popular will." Smith maintained that the "deepest conviction that any Congressman in this democracy ever has is that the will of the people ought to prevail."

Seemingly contrary to the Wahlke-Eulau four-state study are the conclusions of James MacGregor Burns in *Congress on Trial*. Wahlke-Eulau et al. had been concerned with a *state* representative's perception of his role as he explained it in scientific interviews. Burns presents his own astute personal observations of both the national representative's perceptions and of his performance. He characterizes the typical Congressman as a diplomatic agent for his constituency; that is, as a Delegate. The typical Congressman, writes Burns, votes in harmony with the well-organized home folks. Always aware of the next election, the Congressman avoids or straddles national issues that seriously divide his supporters, while always protecting local rights. He is not "a man of political principle." He "spurns the national platform of his party. . . ." He feels that it is his duty to represent his District's interest first.

Burns' observations about the Delegate role of the representative is reinforced by three nation-wide polls taken in 1939 and 1940. In contrast to a 1938 *Fortune* poll, the national sample voted, in 3 Gallup polls in 1939 and 1940, 61%, 66%, and 63% in support of the view that the Congressman should vote according to the way the majority in his district feels. (See "The People Prefer Delegates" below).

The Representative as a Partisan

A third model presented herein—that of the representative as a responsible *Partisan,* a thoughtful advocate of party responsibility— is illustrated by former Vice President Henry Wallace. He held that the member of Congress, on penalty of loss of important committee assignments and party patronage, should support certain basic policies selected by his party's leaders from the party's convention platform. Only in this way, Wallace argued, could the representative be held responsible for his actions and could the voter make an intelligent and effective choice on election day between party programs.

The role of the representative as a responsible party member achieved notable support in a 1950 report of the Committee on Political Parties of the American Political Science Association, entitled, "Toward a More Responsible Two-Party System." Although the authors of this report did not focus specifically on the role of the representative, their report made a strong case for a democratic, responsible, and effective two-party system in which, by clear implication, the representative should follow the party on key issues.

The role of the representative as a Partisan does not rank high in the representative's own perception of his role at the state level. For Congressmen, Burns suggested, the local party is more important than the national party. However, how significant is party pressure on the Congressman? Julius Turner in his analysis of roll calls in *Party and Constituency: Pressures on Congress,* concluded that Congressmen are partisans frequently and significantly. Although Turner's study is more an attempt to measure party cohesion in Congress than to determine if Congressmen are, or see themselves as, party men, his study—if valid—underscores the significant partisan role of the representative. While noting, too, the great pressures of constituencies, Turner held that "the great majority of congressmen . . . yield . . . especially to the pressures of party in casting their votes."

The Representative as Politico

The fourth model we have identified is that of the representative as a *Politico*. This position, like the others, is not always easy to identify in its pure form. A certain amount of balancing of conscience, constituency, and party goes on in all the "ideal-types" we have identified. Yet for purposes of analysis it is possible to isolate that representative who refuses to be pigeon-holed, who insists upon the need, depending upon conditions, to juggle several different roles, and to shift from one to another as circumstances demand. The selection from Robert Luce's *Congress: An Explanation* illustrates this type. Luce, himself a Congressman for many years, wrote that the "lawmaker is not purely an agent, vainly trying to decide what the majority of his principals desire. He is not to be purely a trustee, making wholly independent decisions, self-conceived and self-sustained. He is to be both agent and trustee as far as may be."

A comparable position was taken by George B. Galloway, staff director for the Joint Congressional Committee on Congressional Reorganization in 1946. The Congressman is neither purely the spineless agent of his constituents nor the godlike trustee of his own concept of the public interest. He both leads and follows. On

most issues he may legitimately compromise with party and constituency, for he must rightly keep his eye on what it takes to get
elected.

Wilder Crane's study of the 1957 Wisconsin legislative assembly
enabled him, significantly, to compare the legislator's perception
of his role with his actual decision. Crane holds that "regardless
of how legislators may answer questions concerning normative concepts of style of representation, all of them are politicos."

Frank J. Sorauf, in his 1958 study of the Pennsylvania legislature, entitled *Party and Representation,* arrived at results that contrast with the findings of Wahlke, Eulau, and associates, and that
seem to provide additional empirical support for the Politico role.
Based upon his Pennsylvania study, Sorauf concluded that the
average legislator seems to balance considerations of constituency,
party, and personal judgment and to make choices on issues, in
the light of these demands, tentatively and cautiously.

Historical and Analytical Perspective

For those who appreciate the value of historical perspective the
volume ends with an article by Charles A. Beard and John D.
Lewis, "Representative Government in Evolution." At the option
of the reader this selection may be read first or last. Beard and
Lewis address themselves to the following queries: (1) Why did
representation come into existence as a political idea and practice?
(2) How did earlier conceptions of representation evolve into
present notions? (3) What have been the several meanings of
representation in Western history? (4) What do we mean by representation today? (5) What factors have affected the changing character of the representative's role? Beard and Lewis appreciate that
the modern role of the democratic representative is under fire
both from the Left and the Right. Generally, those on the Right
seek to limit, while those on the Left seek to enhance, the power
of the people.

Ironically, Jean Jacques Rousseau, a foremost radical spokes-
man on behalf of popular sovereignty in the modern world, did
not believe that popular sovereignty and representative government were compatible. He held that "the moment a people allows
itself to be represented, it is no longer free. . . ." Rousseau argued
that sovereignty resides in the people, who, acting under the
General Will, are always right. No representative can make law
on their behalf. Their sovereign power to make law was inalien-

able. It could be given to no one. "The deputies of the people, therefore, are not and cannot be its representatives: they are merely its stewards, and can carry through no definitive acts. Every law the people has not ratified in person is null and void—is, in fact, not a law." Rousseau took an extreme, a polar, position on the question of representation. "The people of England regards itself as free," he wrote in *The Social Contract,* "but it is grossly mistaken; it is free only during the election of members to parliament. As soon as they are elected, slavery overtakes it, and it is nothing." Those who share Rousseau's belief in popular sovereignty now usually accept representative government, but they may still insist that the people's representatives in government do the bidding, reflect the will, of the people.

At the opposite pole from Rousseau are those authoritarians who believe that the people are ignorant, stupid, crass, and lacking in the ability to exercise freedom, directly, or indirectly, through their representatives. Some, like the Grand Inquisitor, in Book V, Chapter 5, of Dostoyevski's *The Brothers Karamazov,* may defend leadership, allegedly on behalf of the people, based on "miracle, mystery, and authority." Like the Fascists, they may advocate authoritarian leadership by which The Leader, *Der Fuehrer, Il Duce,* is the true representative of the people, and shapes the people in his own image, according to his own view of the nation's welfare. The Leader knows best. He is contemptuous of the ability of the masses to rule themselves. He is hostile to parliaments which talk and do not act. He is opposed to majority rule, and to the clash and accommodation of selfish and weak individuals and interests in a constitutional legislative body. By fraud, violence, deception, propaganda the Leader gets the support of the masses and makes them do what he wants and what he maintains is for their best interest. Like the Grand Inquisitor, he will take care of their needs and ensure their happiness.

The selections in this volume on traditional democratic representation, largely in the United States, may be understood better as they are contrasted to these polar positions outlined above.

The conflict of ethical opinion, scientific finding, and prudential judgment reflected in this volume may stimulate the reader to probe more fully the central question herein: *How do we understand the role of the representative in modern America?* Hopefully, he may start with an answer in the United States, move on to other democratic nations, and perhaps conclude with authoritarian nations on the Left and Right. The central problem of this volume will, moreover, lead to such related queries as the meaning of democracy, democratic values in conflict, the process of elections, the behavior of interest groups, the role of party, the performance of the legislative system, the character of leadership, the operation of a federal system, the functioning of public opinion, the democratic politics of compromise. It will lead, in brief, into the heart of American politics.

I Styles of Representation

THE REPRESENTATIVE AS TRUSTEE

EDMUND BURKE

Our Conscience Is a Trust from Providence

Edmund Burke, 1729–1797, was a political philosopher and statesman in the great English Whig tradition. He served in Parliament between 1766 and 1794. Although never a cabinet member himself, he acted as private Secretary to Lord Rockingham, First Lord of the Treasury, and was influential behind governmental scenes. He was an enlightened friend of the American Revolution and a bitter opponent of the French Revolution. The latter revolution was the occasion for his famous attack, Reflections on the Revolution in France *(1789). For this and comparable writings Burke has gained a reputation as the "Father of Modern Conservatism." Although Burke was an astute practical politician, he writes in the grand tradition of his literary and artistic friends, David Garrick, Joshua Reynolds, and Samuel Johnson. Burke made this speech on November 3, 1774. He was elected as a member of Parliament from Bristol for a six-year term.*

. . . I OWE MYSELF, in all things, to *all* the freemen of this city. My particular friends have a demand on me that I should not

From Edmund Burke, "Speech to the Electors of Bristol," *Writings and Speeches of Edmund Burke* (Little, Brown & Co., 1901), Vol. II, pp. 93–98.

deceive their expectations. Never was cause or man supported with more constancy, more activity, more spirit. I have been supported with a zeal, indeed, and heartiness in my friends, which (if their object had been at all proportioned to their endeavors) could never be sufficiently commended. They supported me upon the most liberal principles. They wished that the members for Bristol should be chosen for the city, and for their country at large, and not for themselves.

So far they are not disappointed. If I possess nothing else, I am sure I possess the temper that is fit for your service. . . .

I shall ever retain, what I now feel, the most perfect and grateful attachment to my friends—and I have no enmities, no resentments. I never can consider fidelity to engagements and constancy in friendships but with the highest approbation, even when those noble qualities are employed against my own pretensions. The gentleman who is not so fortunate as I have been in this contest enjoys, in this respect, a consolation full of honor both to himself and to his friends. They have certainly left nothing undone for his service. . . .

I am sorry I cannot conclude without saying a word on a topic touched upon by my worthy colleague.[1] I wish that topic had been passed by at a time when I have so little leisure to discuss it. But since he has thought proper to throw it out, I owe you a clear explanation of my poor sentiments on that subject.

He tells you that "the topic of instructions has occasioned much altercation and uneasiness in this city"; and he expresses himself (if I understand him rightly) in favor of the coercive authority of such instructions.

Certainly, Gentlemen, it ought to be the happiness and glory of a representative to live in the strictest union, the closest correspondence, and the most unreserved communication with his constituents. Their wishes ought to have great weight with him; their opinions high respect; their business unremitted attention. It is his duty to sacrifice his repose, his pleasure, his satisfactions, to theirs —and above all, ever, and in all cases, to prefer their interest to his own.

But his unbiased opinion, his mature judgment, his enlightened conscience, he ought not to sacrifice to you, to any man, or to any set of men living. These he does not derive from your pleasure—no, nor from the law and the constitution. They are a

---

[1] This "worthy" colleague was Henry Cruger who also had been elected for Bristol [Editor].

trust from Providence, for the abuse of which he is deeply answerable. Your representative owes you, not his industry only, but his judgment; and he betrays, instead of serving you, if he sacrifices it to your opinion.

My worthy colleague says his will ought to be subservient to yours. If that be all, the thing is innocent. If government were a matter of will upon any side, yours, without question, ought to be superior. But government and legislation are matters of reason and judgment, and not of inclination; and what sort of reason is that in which the determination precedes the discussion, in which one set of men deliberate and another decide, and where those who form the conclusion are perhaps three hundred miles distant from those who hear the arguments?

To deliver an opinion is the right of all men; that of constituents is a weighty and respectable opinion, which a representative ought always to rejoice to hear, and which he ought always most seriously to consider. But *authoritative* instructions, *mandates* issued, which a member is bound blindly and implicitly to obey, to vote, and to argue for, though contrary to the clearest conviction of his judgment and conscience; these are things utterly unknown to the laws of this land, and which arise from a fundamental mistake of the whole order and tenor of our constitution.

Parliament is not a *congress* of ambassadors from different and hostile interests, which interests each must maintain, as an agent and advocate, against other agents and advocates; but Parliament is a *deliberative* assembly of *one* nation, with *one* interest, that of the whole—where not local purposes, not local prejudices, ought to guide, but the general good, resulting from the general reason of the whole. You choose a member, indeed; but when you have chosen him he is not a member of Bristol, but he is a member of *Parliament*. If the local constituent should have an interest or should form a hasty opinion evidently opposite to the real good of the rest of the community, the member for that place ought to be as far as any other from any endeavor to give it effect. . . . Your faithful friend, your devoted servant, I shall be to the end of my life: a flatterer you do not wish for. . . .

From the first hour I was encouraged to court your favor, to this happy day of obtaining it, I have never promised you anything but humble and persevering endeavors to do my duty. The weight of that duty, I confess, makes me tremble; and whoever well considers what it is, of all things in the world, will fly from

what has the least likeness to a positive and precipitate engage-
ment. To be a good member of Parliament is, let me tell you, no
easy task—especially at this time, when there is so strong a dis-
position to run into the perilous extremes of servile compliance
or wild popularity. To unite circumspection with vigor is abso-
lutely necessary, but it is extremely difficult. We are now members
for a rich commercial *city;* this city, however, is but a part of a
rich commercial *nation,* the interests of which are various, multi-
form, and intricate. We are members for that great nation, which,
however, is itself but part of a great *empire,* extended by our virtue and our fortune to the farthest limits of the East and of the
West. All these wide-spread interests must be considered—must
be compared—must be reconciled, if possible. We are members
for a *free* country; and surely we all know that the machine of a
free constitution is no simple thing, but as intricate and as deli-
cate as it is valuable. We are members in a great and ancient
monarchy; and we must preserve religiously the true, legal rights
of the sovereign, which form the keystone that binds together the
noble and well-constructed arch of our empire and our constitution. . . .

JOHN F. KENNEDY

The Voters Respect Our Independent Judgment

John Fitzgerald Kennedy, 1917–1963, served as a member of the House of Representatives from 1947 to 1953, and as a U.S. Senator from 1953–61, before being elected President of the United States in 1960. He wrote Why England Slept *in 1940, served in the U.S. Navy during World War II, and authored* Profiles in Courage *in 1956. Among his other books are* Strategy of Peace *(1960) and* To Turn the Tide *(1961).*

A NATION WHICH HAS FORGOTTEN the quality of courage which in the past has been brought to public life is not as likely to insist upon or reward that quality in its chosen leaders today—and in fact we have forgotten. We may remember how John Quincy Adams became President through the political schemes of Henry Clay, but we have forgotten how, as a young man, he gave up a promising Senatorial career to stand by the nation. We may remember Daniel Webster for his subservience to the National Bank throughout much of his career, but we have forgotten his sacrifice for the national good at the close of that career. We do not remember—and possibly we do not care.

"People don't give a damn," a syndicated columnist told millions of readers not so many years ago, "what the average Senator or Congressman says. The reason they don't care is that they know what you hear in Congress is 99% tripe, ignorance and demagoguery and not to be relied upon. . . ."

Earlier a member of the Cabinet had recorded in his diary:

While I am reluctant to believe in the total depravity of the Senate, I place but little dependence on the honesty and truthfulness of a large

From pp. 21–30, 31–37 "Courage and Politics" from *Profiles in Courage* by John F. Kennedy. Copyright © 1956 by John F. Kennedy.

portion of the Senators. A majority of them are small lights, mentally weak, and wholly unfit to be Senators. Some are vulgar demagogues . . . some are men of wealth who have purchased their position . . . [some are] men of narrow intellect, limited comprehension, and low partisan prejudice. . . .

And still earlier a member of the Senate itself told his colleagues that "the confidence of the people is departing from us, owing to our unreasonable delays."

The Senate knows that many Americans today share these sentiments. Senators, we hear, must be politicians—and politicians must be concerned only with winning votes, not with statesmanship or courage. Mothers may still want their favorite sons to grow up to be President, but, according to a famous Gallup poll of some years ago, they do not want them to become politicians in the process.

Does this current rash of criticism and disrespect mean the quality of the Senate has declined? Certainly not. For of the three statements quoted above, the first was made in the twentieth century, the second in the nineteenth and the third in the eighteenth (when the first Senate, barely underway, was debating where the Capitol should be located).

Does it mean, then, that the Senate can no longer boast of men of courage?

Walter Lippmann, after nearly half a century of careful observation, rendered in his recent book a harsh judgment both on the politician and the electorate:

With exceptions so rare they are regarded as miracles of nature, successful democratic politicians are insecure and intimidated men. They advance politically only as they placate, appease, bribe, seduce, bamboozle, or otherwise manage to manipulate the demanding threatening elements in their constituencies. The decisive consideration is not whether the proposition is good but whether it is popular—not whether it will work well and prove itself, but whether the active-talking constituents like it immediately.

I am not so sure, after nearly ten years of living and working in the midst of "successful democratic politicians," that they are all "insecure and intimidated men." I am convinced that the complication of public business and the competition for the public's attention have obscured innumerable acts of political courage—large and small—performed almost daily in the Senate Chamber. I am convinced that the decline—if there has been a decline—has been less in the Senate than in the public's appreciation of the art of politics, of the nature and necessity for compromise and balance, and of the nature of the Senate as a legislative chamber. And, finally, I am convinced that we have criticized those who have followed the crowd—and at the same time criticized those who have defied it—because we have not fully understood the responsibility of a Senator to his constituents or recognized the difficulty facing a politician conscientiously desiring, in Webster's words, "to push [his] skiff from the shore alone" into a hostile and turbulent sea. Perhaps if the American people more fully comprehended the terrible pressures which discourage acts of political courage, which drive a Senator to abandon or subdue his conscience, then they might be less critical of those who take the easier road—and more appreciative of those still able to follow the path of courage.

The *first* pressure to be mentioned is a form of pressure rarely recognized by the general public. Americans want to be liked—and Senators are no exception. They are by nature—and of necessity—social animals. We enjoy the comradeship and approval of our friends and colleagues. We prefer praise to abuse, popularity to contempt. Realizing that the path of the conscientious insurgent must frequently be a lonely one, we are anxious to get along with our fellow legislators, our fellow members of the club, to abide by the clubhouse rules and patterns, not to pursue a unique and independent course which would embarrass or irritate the other members. We realize, moreover, that our influence in the club—and the extent to which we can accomplish our objectives and those of our constituents—are dependent in some measure on the esteem with which we are regarded by other Senators. "The way to get along," I was told when I entered Congress, "is to go along."

Going along means more than just good fellowship—it includes the use of compromise, the sense of things possible. We should not be too hasty in condemning all compromise as bad morals. For politics and legislation are not matters for inflexible principles or unattainable ideals. Politics, as John Morley has acutely observed, "is a field where action is one long second best, and where the choice constantly lies between two blunders"; and legislation, under the democratic way of life and the Federal system of Government, requires compromise between the desires of each individual and group and those around them. Henry Clay, who should have known, said compromise was the cement that held the Union together:

All legislation . . . is founded upon the principle of mutual concession. . . . Let him who elevates himself above humanity, above its weaknesses, its infirmities, its wants, its necessities, say, if he pleases, "I never will compromise"; but let no one who is not above the frailties of our common nature disdain compromise.

It is compromise that prevents each set of reformers—the wets and the drys, the one-worlders and the isolationists, the vivisectionists and the anti-vivisectionists—from crushing the group on the extreme opposite end of the political spectrum. The fanatics and extremists and even those conscientiously devoted to hard and fast principles are always disappointed at the failure of their Government to rush to implement all of their principles and to denounce those of their opponents. But the legislator has some responsibility to conciliate those opposing forces within his state and party and to represent them in the larger clash of interests on the national level; and he alone knows that there are few if any issues where all the truth and all the right and all the angels are on one side.

Some of my colleagues who are criticized today for lack of forthright principles—or who are looked upon with scornful eyes as compromising "politicians"—are simply engaged in the fine art of conciliating, balancing and interpreting the forces and factions of public opinion, an art essential to keeping our nation united and enabling our Government to function. Their consciences may direct them from time to time to take a more rigid stand for principle—but their intellects tell them that a fair or poor bill is better than no bill at all, and that only through the give-and-take of compromise will any bill receive the successive approval of the Senate, the House, the President and the nation.

But the question is how we will compromise and with whom. For it is easy to seize upon unnecessary concessions, not as means of legitimately resolving conflicts but as methods of "going along."

There were further implications in the warning that I should "go along"—implications of the rewards that would follow fulfillment of my obligation to follow the party leadership whom I had helped select. All of us in the Congress are made fully aware of the importance of party unity (what sins have been committed in that name!) and the adverse effect upon our party's chances in the next election which any rebellious conduct might bring. Moreover, in these days of Civil Service, the loaves and fishes of patronage available to the legislator—for distribution to those earnest campaigners whose efforts were inspired by something more than mere conviction—are comparatively few; and he who breaks the party's ranks may find that there are suddenly none at all. Even the success of legislation in which he is interested depends in part on the extent to which his support of his party's programs has won him the assistance of his party's leaders. Finally, the Senator who follows the independent course of conscience is likely to discover that he has earned the disdain not only of his colleagues in the Senate and his associates in his party but also that of the all-important contributors to his campaign fund.

It is thinking of that next campaign—the desire to be reelected—that provides the *second* pressure on the conscientious Senator. It should not automatically be assumed that this is a wholly selfish motive—although it is not unnatural that those who have chosen politics as their profession should seek to continue their careers—for Senators who go down to defeat in a vain defense of a single principle will not be on hand to fight for that or any other principle in the future.

Defeat, moreover, is not only a setback for the Senator himself—he is also obligated to consider the effect upon the party he supports, upon the friends and supporters who have "gone out on a limb" for him or invested their savings in his career, and even upon the wife and children whose happiness and security—often depending at least in part upon his success in office—may mean more to him than anything else.

Where else, in a non-totalitarian country, but in the political profession is the individual expected to sacrifice all—including his own career—for the national good? In private life, as in industry, we expect the individual to advance his own enlightened self-interest—within the limitations of the law—in order to achieve over-all progress. But in public life we expect individuals to sacrifice their private interests to permit the national good to progress.

In no other occupation but politics is it expected that a man will sacrifice honors, prestige and his chosen career on a single issue. Lawyers, businessmen, teachers, doctors, all face difficult personal decisions involving their integrity—but few, if any, face them in the glare of the spotlight as do those in public office. Few, if any, face the same dread finality of decision that confronts a Senator facing an important call of the roll. He may want more time for his decision—he may believe there is something to be said for both sides—he may feel that a slight amendment could remove all difficulties—but when that roll is called he cannot hide, he cannot equivocate, he cannot delay—and he senses that his constituency, like the Raven in Poe's poem, is perched there in his Senate desk, croaking "Nevermore" as he casts the vote that stakes his political future.

Few Senators "retire to Pocatello" by choice. The virus of Potomac Fever, which rages everywhere in Washington, breeds nowhere in more virulent form than on the Senate floor. The prospect of forced retirement from "the most exclusive club in the world," the possibilities of giving up the interesting work, the fascinating trappings and the impressive prerogatives of Congressional office, can cause even the most courageous politician serious loss of sleep. Thus, perhaps without realizing it, some Senators tend to take the easier, less troublesome path to harmonize or rationalize what at first appears to be a conflict between their conscience—or the result of their deliberations—and the majority opinion of their constituents. Such Senators are not political cowards—they have simply developed the habit of sincerely reaching conclusions inevitably in accordance with popular opinion.

Still other Senators have not developed that habit—they have neither conditioned nor subdued their consciences—but they feel, sincerely and without cynicism, that they must leave considerations of conscience aside if they are to be effective. The profession of politics, they would agree with political writer Frank Kent, is not immoral, simply nonmoral:

> Probably the most important single accomplishment for the politically ambitious is the fine art of seeming to say something without doing so. . . . The important thing is not to be on the right side of the current issue but on the popular side . . . regardless of your own convictions or of the facts. This business of getting the votes is a severely practical one into which matters of morality, of right and wrong, should not be allowed to intrude.

And Kent quotes the advice allegedly given during the 1920 campaign by former Senator Ashurst of Arizona to his colleague Mark Smith:

Mark, the great trouble with you is that you refuse to be a demagogue. You will not submerge your principles in order to get yourself elected. *You must learn that there are times when a man in public life is compelled to rise above his principles.*

Not all Senators would agree—but few would deny that the desire to be re-elected exercises a strong brake on independent courage.

The *third* and most significant source of pressures which discourage political courage in the conscientious Senator or Congressman—and practically all of the problems described in this chapter apply equally to members of both Houses—is the pressure of his constituency, the interest groups, the organized letter writers, the economic blocs and even the average voter. To cope with such pressures, to defy them or even to satisfy them, is a formidable task. All of us occasionally have the urge to follow the example of Congressman John Steven McGroarty of California, who wrote a constituent in 1934:

One of the countless drawbacks of being in Congress is that I am compelled to receive impertinent letters from a jackass like you in which you say I promised to have the Sierra Madre mountains reforested and I have been in Congress two months and haven't done it. Will you please take two running jumps and go to hell.

Fortunately, or unfortunately, few follow that urge—but the provocation is there—not only from unreasonable letters and impossible requests, but also from hopelessly inconsistent demands and endlessly unsatisfied grievances. . . .

All of us in the Senate meet endless examples of such conflicting pressures, which only reflect the inconsistencies inevitable in our complex economy. If we tell our constituents frankly that we can do nothing, they feel we are unsympathetic or inadequate. If we try and fail—usually meeting a counteraction from other Senators representing other interests—they say we are like all the rest of the politicians. All we can do is retreat into the Cloakroom and weep on the shoulder of a sympathetic colleague—or go home and snarl at our wives.

We may tell ourselves that these pressure groups and letter writers represent only a small percentage of the voters—and this is true. But they are the articulate few whose views cannot be ignored and who constitute the greater part of our contacts with the public at large, whose opinions we cannot know, whose vote we must obtain and yet who in all probability have a limited idea of what we are trying to do. (One Senator, since retired, said that he voted with the special interests on every issue, hoping that by election time all of them added together would constitute nearly a majority that would remember him favorably, while the other members of the public would never know about—much less remember—his vote against their welfare. It is reassuring to know that this seemingly unbeatable formula did not work in his case.)

These, then, are some of the pressures which confront a man of conscience. He cannot ignore the pressure groups, his constituents, his party, the comradeship of his colleagues, the needs of his family, his own pride in office, the necessity for compromise and the importance of remaining in office. He must judge for himself which path to choose, which step will most help or hinder the ideals to which he is committed. He realizes that once he begins to weigh each issue in terms of his chances for re-election, once he begins to compromise away his principles on one issue after another for fear that to do otherwise would halt his career and prevent future fights for principle, then he has lost the very freedom of conscience which justifies his continuance in office. But to decide at which point and on which issue he will risk his career is a difficult and soul-searching decision.

But this is no real problem, some will say. Always do what is right, regardless of whether it is popular. Ignore the pressures, the temptations, the false compromises.

That is an easy answer—but it is easy only for those who do not bear the responsibilities of elected office. For more is involved than pressure, politics and personal ambitions. Are we rightfully entitled to ignore the demands of our constituents even if we are able and willing to do so? We have noted the pressures that make political courage a difficult course—let us turn now to those Constitutional and more theoretical obligations which cast doubt upon the propriety of such a course—obligations to our state and section, to our party, and above all, to our constituents.

The primary responsibility of a Senator, most people assume, is to represent the views of his state. Ours is a Federal system—a Union of relatively sovereign states whose needs differ greatly—and my Constitutional obligations as Senator would thus appear to require me to represent the interests of my state. Who will speak for Massachusetts if her own Senators do not? Her rights and even her identity become submerged. Her equal representation in Congress is lost. Her aspirations, however much they may from time to time be in the minority, are denied that equal opportunity to be heard to which all minority views are entitled.

Any Senator need not look very long to realize that his colleagues are representing *their* local interests. And if such interests are ever to be abandoned in favor of the national good, let the constituents —not the Senator—decide when and to what extent. For he is their agent in Washington, the protector of their rights, recognized by the Vice President in the Senate Chamber as "the Senator from Massachusetts" or "the Senator from Texas."

But when all of this is said and admitted, we have not yet told the full story. For in Washington we are "United States Senators" and members of the Senate of the United States as well as Senators from Massachusetts and Texas. Our oath of office is administered by the Vice President, not by the Governors of our respective states; and we come to Washington, to paraphrase Edmund Burke, not as hostile ambassadors or special pleaders for our state or section, in opposition to advocates and agents of other areas, but as members of the deliberative assembly of one nation with one interest. Of course, we should not ignore the needs of our area— nor could we easily as products of that area—but none could be found to look out for the national interest if local interests wholly dominated the role of each of us.

There are other obligations in addition to those of state and region—the obligations of the party whose pressures have already been described. Even if I can disregard those pressures, do I not have an obligation to go along with the party that placed me in office? We believe in this country in the principle of party responsibility, and we recognize the necessity of adhering to party platforms—if the party label is to mean anything to the voters. Only in this way can our basically two-party nation avoid the pitfalls of multiple splinter parties—whose purity and rigidity of principle, I might add—if I may suggest a sort of Gresham's Law of politics—increase inversely with the size of their membership.

And yet we cannot permit the pressures of party responsibility to submerge on every issue the call of personal responsibility. For the party which, in its drive for unity, discipline and success, ever decides to exclude new ideas, independent conduct or insurgent members, is in danger. In the words of Senator Albert Beveridge:

A party can live only by growing, intolerance of ideas brings its death. . . . An organization that depends upon reproduction only for its vote, son taking the place of father, is not a political party, but a Chinese tong; not citizens brought together by thought and conscience, but an Indian tribe held together by blood and prejudice.

The two-party system remains not because both are rigid but because both are flexible. The Republican party when I entered Congress was big enough to hold, for example, both Robert Taft and Wayne Morse—and the Democratic side of the Senate in which I now serve can happily embrace, for example, both Harry Byrd and Wayne Morse.

Of course, both major parties today seek to serve the national interest. They would do so in order to obtain the broadest base of support, if for no nobler reason. But when party and officeholder differ as to how the national interest is to be served, we must place first the responsibility we owe not to our party or even to our constituents but to our individual consciences.

But it is a little easier to dismiss one's obligations to local interests and party ties than to face squarely the problem of one's responsibility to the will of his constituents. A Senator who avoids this responsibility would appear to be accountable to no one, and the basic safeguards of our democratic system would thus have vanished. He is no longer representative in the true sense, he has violated his public trust, he has betrayed the confidence demonstrated by those who voted for him to carry out their views. "Is the creature," as John Tyler asked the House of Representatives in his maiden speech, "to set himself in opposition to his Creator? Is the servant to disobey the wishes of his master?"

How can he be regarded as representing the people when he speaks, not their language, but his own? He ceases to be their representative when he does so, and represents himself alone.

In short, according to this school of thought, if I am to be properly responsive to the will of my constituents, it is my duty to place their principles, not mine, above all else. This may not always be easy, but it nevertheless is the essence of democracy, faith in the wisdom of the people and their views. To be sure, the people will make mistakes—they will get no better government than they deserve—but that is far better than the representative of the people arrogating for himself the right to say he knows better than they what is good for them. Is he not chosen, the argument closes, to vote as they would vote were they in his place?

It is difficult to accept such a narrow view of the role of United States Senator—a view that assumes the people of Massachusetts sent me to Washington to serve merely as a seismograph to record shifts in popular opinion. I reject this view not because I lack faith in the "wisdom of the people," but because this concept of democracy actually puts too little faith in the people. Those who would deny the obligation of the representative to be bound by every impulse of the electorate—regardless of the conclusions his own deliberations direct—do trust in the wisdom of the people. They have faith in their ultimate sense of justice, faith in their ability to honor courage and respect judgment, and faith that in the long run they will act unselfishly for the good of the nation. It is that kind of faith on which democracy is based, not simply the often frustrated hope that public opinion will at all times under all circumstances promptly identify itself with the public interest.

The voters selected us, in short, because they had confidence in our judgment and our ability to exercise that judgment from a position where we could determine what were their own best interests, as a part of the nation's interests. This may mean that we must on occasion lead, inform, correct and sometimes even ignore constituent opinion, if we are to exercise fully that judgment for which we were elected. But acting without selfish motive or private bias, those who follow the dictates of an intelligent conscience are not aristocrats, demagogues, eccentrics or callous politicians insensitive to the feelings of the public. They expect—and not without considerable trepidation—their constituents to be the final judges of the wisdom of their course; but they have faith that those constituents—today, tomorrow or even in another generation—will at least respect the principles that motivated their independent stand.

JOHN C. WAHLKE, HEINZ EULAU, *et al.*

The Trustee Orientation
Is Most Realistic

*John C. Wahlke is Professor of Political Science at the
University of Iowa. He is the co-author of* Legislative
Behavior *(1962) and* Government and Politics *(1966).
Heinz Eulau is Professor of Political Science at Stanford
University. He is the author of* The Behavioral Persua-
sion in Politics *(1962) and co-author of* Lawyers in Poli-
tics *(1964).* William Buchanan *teaches at the University
of Tennessee and is co-author of* How Nations See Each
Other *(1953) and of* An International Police Force and
Public Opinion *(1954).* LeRoy Ferguson *is Professor of
Political Science at Michigan State University. He is
co-author of* Politics in the Press *(1954).*

Perceptions of the Representational Role

REPRESENTATIONAL-ROLE orientations were derived from responses
to the following two questions:

> How would you describe the job of being a legislator—what are
> the most important things you should do here?
> Are there any important differences between what you think this
> job is and the way your constituents see it?

Responses to these questions yielded three major representational-
role orientations: trustee, delegate, and politico. In the following
we shall describe these orientational types as they were defined by
legislators themselves.

Trustee. The role orientation of trustee finds expression in two
major conceptions of how decisions ought to be made. These conceptions may occur severally and jointly. There is, first, a moralistic

From John C. Wahlke *et al., The Legislative System* (New York, 1962), pp. 272–282, 285–
286. Reprinted by permission of John Wiley & Sons, Inc., Publishers.

interpretation. The trustee sees himself as a free agent in that, as a premise of his decision-making behavior, he claims to follow what he considers right or just, his convictions and principles, the dictates of his conscience. In proceeding along this path of moral righteousness, trustees may give different "reasons" for their interpretation of this role. First, the trustee's ideas, attitudes, or legislative objectives are in harmony with those of the represented. And because they are in harmony, he need not pay attention to instructions—for no instructions are forthcoming, and he can follow the dictates of his conscience:

> No, there are no differences between my idea of the job and that of the type of people I represent. They accept my philosophy which I have frequently expressed to them. Once when I was campaigning one of my constituents came up and asked if I had voted so that I would get sent back. I told him no, I voted the way I felt was right.
> I have never been under pressure once to go against my convictions. I've always stuck to them and I've won more friends than I've lost. I feel I have the confidence of my constituents so that when a problem comes up, I will make a decision that will be in accordance with their best interests.

Secondly, the trustee claims that he must fall back on his own principles in making decisions because those from whom he might take cues—constituents, lobbyists, leaders, or colleagues—cannot be trusted:

> His most important and difficult job is to vote according to his conscience without letting other things interfere—even his own constituents. They are axe-grinding elements.
> No, wherever differences do exist, you'll get along if you do what you know is right—they usually go along with it. Sometimes you get complaints, but they're usually just emotional appeals which you should be suspicious of: they should be avoided. You shouldn't waver in your convictions because of them.

Finally, if the representative as a man of principle finds himself in conflict with the represented, he should not submit but try to persuade them to his convictions. The trustee here sees himself as a "mentor." He is not in agreement with his constituents, but he does not turn his back on them. Sticking to his ideas, he tries to bring others around to his point of view:

There are often personal differences. The people in the district often express their views one way. It's best to do what you feel should be done. I usually go by my own convictions and depend on being able to convince them when I get back that I did the right things.

There is also a judgmental conception of the role of trustee. The trustee is not bound by a mandate because his decisions are his own considered judgments based on an assessment of the facts in each decision, his understanding of all the problems and angles involved, his thoughtful appraisal of the sides at issue. He may feel that he must follow his own judgments because the community from which he comes expects him to do so:

There are two theories of representation. The first is the delegate theory. Here you are the voice of the community from which you come. Then there is the representative theory. That is, the man is elected for his own capabilities in the solution of problems. I am inclined to this theory. I would say that my community is also of this mind.

Or, representation may be spontaneous in this conception, a product of agreement between representative and represented without any active communication of opinions or beliefs. The representative shares the outlook of his constituents:

As to what should be accomplished here, I think it should be what I think should be done rather than the people here. I've lived in this town 39 years, and you think like the town does. They might show me that this isn't true, but until I find out I assume that they feel the same way as I do.

Or the trustee may follow his own judgment because he cannot afford to allow himself to be influenced by persons who are committed or ill informed:

The most important job is . . . an ability to reach decisions, to solve problems without being unduly influenced by the feelings of persons who are committed or paid, or who for lack of information or ability are incapable of reaching a decision. I do not consider myself as a delegate. People are not capable to tell me what to do—not because they are stupid, but because they have limited access to the facts. If they had the facts, their decision would be the same.

The crucial point in this response is, of course, that if people had the facts, their judgment would be the same as that of the representative. But the theme that constituents and others are ill informed because they have no access to the facts in terms of which decisions must be made is recurrent:

I spend a lot of time looking at both sides. I have the time to do it. People back home are busy and see only one side. My job is to check all angles of a problem, and they want me to use my best judgment.

I think I'm elected by the people to be their representative, and they must have confidence in my judgment, assuming that I have studied the situation in making my decisions. I can't please everyone all the time, even my best friends. I believe in a republican form of government. You elect people to represent you and then abide by their decisions. If they make too many wrong decisions, you elect others. There is a tendency in some cases by some people to return all decisions to the people. I'm not in agreement with that: it's not that they are incapable, but that they don't take time to inform themselves. It's not true of all, but the majority do this.

A related view sees the trustee role as inevitable not because the represented do not understand the problems which the representative faces, but because the representative cannot find out the preferences of his clientele, even if he tried to do so. He must, therefore, fall back on his own judgment:

Well, of course, I have never subscribed to the theory that I'm here to reflect the views of my constituents. I'm here to vote as I see it. You can't vote by what you think the constituents' thinking is. You don't know what that thinking is. Even if you receive 100 letters on a bill, this is a very small proportion in respect to the size of the district. . . . A bill might be opposed by interests which I represent, but if I personally agree with the bill, then I will follow my principles, even if they don't agree with certain Republican interests which might have contributed to my election.

But his own difficulty in ascertaining constituents' preferences, or the clientele's lack of information, does not mean that the trustee should be oblivious of the ideas or opinions of others. He may listen before arriving at a decision:

He should regard the laws for which there seems a need partly in the light of public opinion, but partly on his own judgment. If he refers only to his constituents, why be here at all? I represent the welfare of my community as I see it. Otherwise they can get another boy. Of course, at times you want advice—if you are not sure what the effect of a proposed law may be. Mostly I prefer to do my own thinking.

I'm open to intelligent ideas from my constituents. I'm not interested in simple notes from them saying "vote yes" or "vote no" on bill X. When I get letters like that I sometimes answer them asking for their reasons so that I may be better able to make my own decisions. They seldom reply.

Finally, it seems to be an important aspect of the trustee's role orientation that he should be willing to accept the political consequences of his refusal to be swayed by public opinion. The trustee may be aware of the implications of his conception of representation for political responsibility:

I found out long ago you can't poll your constituents. You can't supply them either with the information so that they can make intelligent decisions. So I haven't concerned myself with them. I try to inform myself and vote as I please. If they don't like it they have a chance to get me at the next election.

I operate on the principle that I'm here to use my own judgment. A representative is good as long as his ideas coincide with the constituents' wishes. If they don't, it's up to them to throw me out, not for me to change. Not that I don't think you should listen to them. Still I think a legislator should do what he thinks best regardless of public opinion. I do pretty much what I think is best. . . . You see guys here who follow the whims of the people. What's wrong with that is that they're not smart enough to figure out what the people think.

Vote your convictions rather than voting for what you think someone else thinks or wants. Let them defeat you if they want, and can. My first year here I tried to ask everyone's point of view and find out how I should vote. But that doesn't work; they don't know themselves what they want. They may tell you to vote for bill 121 but after talking to them you find out that what they really want would not be accomplished by the bill. Now I vote for what I think they want. I don't ask them anymore. I do it for them.

Evidently, a great variety of conceptions of representation are involved in the role orientation of the trustee. In particular, it seems that this orientation derives not only from a normative definition of the role of the representative, but that it is also often grounded in interpersonal situations which make it functionally inevitable. The condition that the represented do not have the information necessary to give intelligent instructions, that the representative is unable to discover what his clientele may want, that preferences remain un-expressed, that there is no need for instructions because of an alleged harmony of interests between representative and represented—all of the circumstances may be acknowledged as sources of the role orientation of trustee, at times even forced on the representative against his own predilection for a mandate if that were possible.

Delegate. Just as the trustee role orientation involves a variety of conceptions of representation, so does the orientation of delegate. All delegates are agreed, of course, that they should not use their independent judgment or principled convictions as decision-making premises. But this does not mean that they feel equally committed to follow instructions, from whatever clientele. Some merely say that they try to inform themselves before making decisions by consulting their constituents or others; however, they seem to imply that such consultation has a mandatory effect on their behavior: "I do ask them (i.e., constituents) quite often, especially where there's doubt in my mind." Others frankly acknowledge instructions as necessary or desirable premises in decision making: "I do what they want me to do. Being re-elected is the best test"; or, "A majority of the people always gets their way with me." More emphatic is this response:

What the district wants me to do is my most important job. I carry out their decisions. I'll put any bill in the hopper they give me. If they wanted me to move this capitol, I'd break my neck to do it.

Finally, there is the representative in the delegate role who not only feels that he should follow instructions, but who also believes that he should do so even if these instructions are explicitly counter to his own judgment or principles: "Some things I'm not particularly sold on, but if the people want it, they should have it"; or, "Reflect the thinking of my district even if it is not my own private thinking." The following two responses are more explicit than most in this connection:

I want to express their views rather than my own. On a controversial matter I'll vote the way I think the majority want even if I personally disagree.

I voted once against my own will to favor my constituents. I wrote a letter to the papers about whether they wanted a State Board of Education appointed or elected, and asked them what they wanted me to do. I favored an appointed board, but they, a preponderance of them, said an elected board. When it came to the decision, I voted for the elected board. I feel that when a fellow represents a section, he should represent their feelings and try to find out their feelings.

What strikes one in these comments, in contrast to those made by trustees, is the failure to elaborate in greater detail the problem of why the representative should follow instructions in his decision-making behavior. Delegates, it seems, have a simpler, more mechanical conception of the political process and of the function of representation in legislative behavior. Perhaps most noticeable, in contrast to the trustee orientation, is the omission of delegates to raise the question of political responsibility under conditions of strict instructions. Apparently, the problem is ignored by the delegate precisely because he rejects the possibility of discretion in his decision making. It is a matter of speculation whether the role orientation of delegate is based on a conscious majoritarian bias which he could elaborate and defend if necessary, or whether it simply reflects lack of political articulation and sophistication. On the other hand, the fact that the delegate seems to have so little doubt about his role suggests that, whatever his reasons and regardless of whether his decisions are really in accord with the views of different groups among his clientele, he is likely to be characterized by a fairly high sense of personal effectiveness in his approach to lawmaking.

Politico. As suggested earlier, the classical dichotomization of the concept of representation in terms of independent judgment and mandate was unlikely to exhaust the empirical possibilities of representational behavior. In particular, it would seem to be possible for a representative to act in line with both criteria. For roles and role orientations need not be mutually exclusive. Depending on circumstances, a representative may hold the role orientation of trustee at one time, and the role orientation of delegate at another time. Or he might even seek to reconcile both orientations in terms of a third. In other words, the representational-role set comprises the extreme orientations of trustee and delegate and a third orientation, the politico, resulting from overlap of these two. Within the orientational range called politico, the trustee and delegate roles may be taken simultaneously, possibly making for role conflict, or they may be taken seriatim, one after another as legislative situations dictate.

Because our data do not permit us to discriminate too sharply between these two possibilities, we shall speak of legislators who express both orientations, either simultaneously or serially, as politicos.[1] In other words, in contrast to either trustees or delegates as relatively "pure" types, representatives holding the role orientation of politico exhibit a certain amount of flexibility in their representational relationships. A qualitative review of the interview protocols may serve to articulate the two possibilities.

Both role orientations—that of trustee and that of delegate—may be held serially, depending on whether the legislator's focus of attention is centered in one clientele or another. For instance, he may see himself as a delegate in matters of local interest, and as a trustee in all other matters:

> As a member there are certain things you should do. First you have a specific responsibility to the people of your own constituency on matters of local interest. Second, you should use your own judgment on all matters pertaining to benefits for the people within the framework of governmental policy and should think of what's best for the state as a whole. It's not necessary to follow the will of the people always as you should decide what most benefits the present and future and hope history proves you right.

Or the legislator may feel that he must follow his party's instructions in political matters, though on others he can be a free agent:

> My conception of party responsibility—there's a responsibility to the party to vote with them, with respect to administration bills—there's responsibility to go along with the governor. On matters removed from the political category I would vote my convictions.

These comments suggest that both the trustee and delegate roles may be taken, depending on the character of the issue involved or the legislator's focus of attention. But no attempt is made to reconcile the two orientations. They coexist side by side and may be invoked as political circumstances require. These legislators do not seem to feel that they are facing a situation which makes for conflict of roles, largely because they succeed in avoiding conflict by not attempting to reconcile the two orientations. As one representative clearly put it:

[1] Provision for such discrimination was made in the coding of responses, but differences among the coders seemed to introduce a good deal of bias in this connection. Hence it seemed preferable to combine these responses in a single category—politico.

Well, that gets you into a major philosophical question. Is it the duty of the representative simply to do what people want, or is it his duty to figure out what's in the best interest of people and state, and persuade them that it is? *Uniformly, I have not taken either one position—sometimes one, sometimes the other. . . .* The evidence of success is that I'm still here.

On the other hand, some legislators may be more sensitive to the potential conflict to which they may be exposed by the ambiguity of the representational relationship and seek to come to grips with it. These representatives are not only aware of the problem, but, instead of solving it by sometimes taking the trustee role, sometimes the delegate role, they seek to balance simultaneously the instructions or preferences of clienteles against their own judgment:

There is a line of demarcation between what they want at home and what you think is good for them. I haven't been too disturbed by that yet but it could become a major problem. I don't think I could ever settle just where the line is. It is too flexible. Each piece of legislation must be considered individually to determine it.

My job is to look after their interests (i.e., of constituents) and carry out what they want done. But this is subject to the limitation that they can't possibly know all I do if I'm doing my job. They are very understanding. I haven't been threatened that if I don't do what they want I won't be reelected.

While these respondents leave the possible resolution of conflict between representational-role orientations open, some politicos tend to resolve it, when the chips are down, in favor of the trustee role:

There is an age-old question—should I vote according to my convictions, or according to the people back home? I think I should follow my convictions but consider the people back home. However, their views are not necessarily best. They get biased views on issues—all of them are members of some pressure groups. A legislator hears both sides. . . . Public opinion is subject to change; it can't be ignored or you won't come back.

A good many think that you should do what the majority wants, regardless of your personal feelings, and I think what you do is to consider their desires as *one* of the elements in arriving at a conclusion. But you also have to consider the other elements presented here. In other words, You are in a better position to see the relative merits of the bill here than they are. The basic question is: are you elected to do what the majority wants or what you think is best?

Finally, there may be an explicit defense of independent judgment as the more important criterion in decision making, precisely because instructions from particular groups have to be integrated in the legislative process. Here the representational role of politico blends smoothly into the purposive role of broker:

> It's difficult to use the term "constituents" to give a composite picture. . . . Particular groups have particular interests that sometimes interfere with the common good. Most constituents feel I am their representative rather than a common representative, and, as a result, I must weigh the conflicting desires of various groups to determine what will benefit the most people in my district. A legislator should realize that in most cases the sincerity and desires of others are just as genuine as his own. He has to try as far as possible—even by giving in sometimes on his own obstinate opinions—to work out the best solution possible without sacrificing principle.

In general, then, the politico as a representational-role taker differs from both the trustee and the delegate in that he seems to be more sensitive to conflicting alternatives, more flexible in the ways in which he tries to resolve the conflict among alternatives, and less dogmatic in his orientation towards legislative behavior as it is related to his representational role. Whether he is or can be successful in performing the role is a matter to which we shall turn later on.

Distribution of Representational-role Orientations

The spell of the Burkean formulation on the interpretation of representation tended to create reactions which, it seems, are almost as arbitrary as Burke's formula itself. In particular, the functional notion, itself quite realistic under modern conditions, that the legislature is an agency for the coordination and integration of diverse social, economic, and political interests makes apparent the simple-mindedness of Burke's theory, now as then. Friedrich, for instance, has pointed out that "the pious formula that representatives are not bound by mandate, that they are subject only to their conscience and are supposed to serve the common weal, which is repeated in so many European constitutions, while significant as a norm, may lead to differentiating as well as to integrative results."[2] Yet, once the

[2] Carl J. Friedrich, *op. cit.,* p. 297.

distinction is made between the style of the representative's role and its focus, Burke's "pious formula" may still be relevant.[3] Both the focus and the style are likely to be influenced by the character of politics at a given time and by the demands of contemporary political circumstances on the representative as a decision maker.

We may, for instance, assume the following: the exigencies of modern government, even on the relatively low level of state government, are exceedingly complex. Taxation and finance, education and public welfare, legal reform, licensing and regulatory problems, transportation, and so on are topics more often than not beyond the comprehension of the average citizen. Unable to understand their problems and helpless to cope with them, people are likely to entrust the affairs of government to the elected representatives who, presumably, are better informed than their constituents. Many of the comments made by trustees about their constituents articulated this set of reasoning. People themselves may pay lip service to the notion that a representative should not use his independent judgment,[4] but in fact they are unlikely to be able, or may not care, to give him instructions as was possibly the case at an earlier time when the tasks of government were comparatively simple. It is likely, therefore, that the representative has become less and less a delegate and more and more a trustee as the business of government has become more and more intricate and technical as well as less locally centered. Rather than being a "pious formula," the role orientation of trustee may be a functional necessity. We might expect, therefore, that it is held by state legislators more frequently today than the role orientation of delegate, with the politico orientation in a middle position.

Comparative analysis of the distribution of representational-role orientations in the four states seems to support these considerations. As Table 1 shows, the role orientation of trustee is held by greater proportions of legislators in all four states than either the politico or delegate orientations. Moreover, the politico appears somewhat more often in all four states than the delegate.

---

[3] *Style* refers to the representative's approach to his task as a political actor—i.e., as a Trustee, Delegate, Partisan, or Politico. *Focus* refers to the area or constituency that is the representative's object of concern—e.g., the Nation, the state of California, his congressional district, or the key interests or pressures involved. [Editor's note.]

[4] See Hadley Cantril, Ed., *Public Opinion, 1935-1946* (Princeton: Princeton University Press, 1951), p. 133.

TABLE 1: DISTRIBUTION OF REPRESENTATIONAL-ROLE ORIENTATIONS

Role Orientation	Calif. $N = 49$	N.J. $N = 54$	Ohio $N = 114$	Tenn. $N = 78$
Trustee	55%	61%	56%	81%
Politico	25	22	29	13
Delegate	20	17	15	6
Total	100%	100%	100%	100%

The trustee orientation, Table 1 indicates, appears more frequently in Tennessee than in the other three states, a fact that seems to contradict the proposition that the orientation of trustee varies with the complexity of governmental affairs. As Tennessee is less urbanized and industrialized than the other states, one might expect Tennessee legislators to be less often trustees and more often delegates than legislators in California, New Jersey, or Ohio. But it may be that "complexity" is a function of perceptions, regardless of the real situation. If so, then to Tennesseans the relatively less complex character of socio-economic life may appear more complex than it actually is, compared with the other states. The more frequent appearance of the trustee there may only be symptomatic of an even greater feeling of helplessness and inefficacy on the part of people vis-á-vis governmental problems, as it is perceived by their representatives. It may also be a reflection of the lower educational level in Tennessee. In all these cases, the political character of Tennessee constituencies would seem to make it very difficult for a legislator to be a delegate for his constituency, forcing him to act as either a trustee or a politico. But to demonstrate this is beyond the limits of this analysis. But the most surprising feature of Table 1 is the very small proportion of legislators in each state subscribing to the role orientation of delegate. If one assumes that the extent to which any role is taken is a function of its difficulty, it would seem that the role orientation of delegate is, indeed, most difficult to hold. We noted in the review of responses regarding different orientations made in the interviews that legislators repeatedly gave as a reason for their taking the role of trustee the fact that it was impossible to find out what people really wanted, and that, therefore, the delegate role was unrealistic. Whether realistic or not, the data reveal that very few legislators took the delegate role. . . .

Conclusion

Three major role orientations—trustee, politico, and delegate—seem to be characteristic of the legislator's representational style, i.e., of how he relates himself to his decision-making behavior. The trustee claims to rely on his own conscience, on what he thinks is right, or on his considered judgment of the facts involved in the issue which he has to decide. The delegate claims that he seeks and follows instructions from his constituents or other clienteles. The politico claims that he will adopt one or the other orientation as conditions call for, and that he must balance one against the other.

Under modern conditions, the trustee orientation is probably more realistic. Given the complexity of governmental problems, on the one hand, and the difficulty of finding out what clienteles may want, the delegate orientation is probably least functional from the point of view of effective representation. In the four states, many more legislators take the role of trustee than the roles of politico or delegate. If extent of role taking is an indication of the degree of difficulty involved in a given role, it would seem that the trustee role is the easiest and the delegate role the most difficult to take.

THE REPRESENTATIVE AS DELEGATE

ALFRED DE GRAZIA

The Representative Ought to Consult the Majority

Alfred de Grazia is Professor of Government at New York University. Among his publications are the following: Human Relations in Public Administration *(1949)*, Elements of Political Science *(1952)*, Propaganda Overseas *(1953)*, Western Public *(1954)*, Elite Analysis *(1955)*, American Way of Government *(1957)*, and Welfare in America *(1960)*. He has also served as Editor of the American Behavioral Scientist.

The following selection, which is not necessarily Professor de Grazia's own position, may be found in his Public and Republic: Political Representation in America *(New York: Knopf, 1951)*.

THE DOCTRINE OF INSTRUCTIONS, which maintains that, at any time, a clear expression of the will of the majority of constituents is binding on the action of their representative, appears with the very beginning of parliamentary representation in England. As long as the constituency was small, legislation was simple, and the power of Parliament was not a general power of legislation and sovereignty, the doctrine was not questioned. When Parliament grew into a sovereign oligarchy, and the electorate became relatively insignificant as an organized power, the doctrine of instructions declined.

From *Public and Republic*, by Alfred de Grazia, pp. 123–127. Copyright 1951 by Alfred A. Knopf, Inc. Reprinted by permission.

It was revived in the Enlightenment as part of the context of individualism and the contractual psychology of the rational democrats, and it became a subject of dispute between Burke and the Radicals, each representing a different theory of society.

In America, the colonists for the most part looked favorably upon the doctrine, and it was not until the post-Revolutionary period that it was challenged by men like Madison and Hamilton. In the First Congress, a proposal was made to include in the Bill of Rights the right to instruct representatives, but the proposal was voted down by a large majority.[1] Most members felt that the provision would be inapplicable to real circumstances, while others believed that the representative must be allowed his independent judgment in deciding on political affairs. The right to petition Congress, declared Madison, gave substantially the power of instructing to the people, without the difficulty of determining the momentary attitude of the majority. If more than advice was intended by the proposal, he stated, the amendment was undesirable.

Two ways of looking at the doctrine are suggested by the debate in Congress. One regards the doctrine in constitutional form as a law to be observed, and therefore the practical objections to be insuperable, for even a representative of the First Congress, with 30,000 constituents, could not know most of the time the sentiments of a majority of his constituents. The second way of approaching the doctrine of instructions is philosophical. Just as several provisions of the various bills of rights being adopted at the time were already covered by existing constitutional safeguards or might better have been covered in their proper place in the constitutions, so might the doctrine of instructions be handled. But, as with the Bill of Rights, more than a law was being stated. An attitude toward political life was being promulgated in sacred form. The doctrine of instructions was to be an ideal.

The ideal would state: "A representative ought to act at all times as if he were consulting the majority will and acting only in accordance with its decision, abolishing all other interests from his mind." Or, as Parke Godwin angrily put it in his *Political Essays:* "A representative is but the mouthpiece and organ of his constituents. What we want in legislation as in other trusts, are honest fiduciaries, men who will perform their duties according to our wishes."[2] The doctrine was a counterpoise to ideas of checks and

---

[1] *Annals of Congress,* Vol. I, pp. 138 ff.
[2] Parke Godwin, *Political Essays* (1856), pp. 40, 41-2.

balances and of minority protection. It reflected a great popular confidence in the majority and a desire to see the wishes of the majority transformed directly into political action, without benefit of constitutional and legal barriers and without interference from minor interests.

As such, the doctrine was rejected by the leaders of national constitutional opinion. It was to be found in some state constitutions, despite the difficulty of conceiving the actual working of the idea. Pennsylvania, in its Constitution of 1776, first declared explicitly the right of instruction.[3] North Carolina[4] and Vermont followed the example. Massachusetts in 1780 stated the principle in even stronger words, and, strangely enough, it was John Adams, the foremost exponent of class government, who was principally responsible for its insertion in the Massachusetts document.[5] New Hampshire followed suit, as did the new states of the Northwest Territory. During the debates in the state conventions over the ratification of the Constitution, the matter was brought up in Virginia and Massachusetts in connection with the instruction of Senators by the legislatures. Both conventions seem to have felt that the states would have that security and so they let the matter pass.

In practice, the judgments of the conventions were vindicated. Although from time to time various opinions were expressed against the practice by which the state legislatures instructed their senators on matters pending on the Senate floor, the instructions of the states were carried out.[6] From the beginning the Massachusetts legislature followed the practice of "instructing" senators and "requesting" representatives; Virginia did the same. Representatives, deriving their authority from direct elections, could not be commanded by the legislature, it was felt. It is notable that, in 1808, when the Massachusetts legislature gave John Quincy Adams instructions against the embargo, he considered himself unable to follow the instructions and resigned his seat. His action was the common one whenever the legislature did not see eye to eye with the senators on an issue and the senators thought the matter too important for them to act in opposition to their convictions.

In several cases, notably those of Pickering of Massachusetts in

[3] Robert Luce, *Legislative Principles* (1930), p. 453.

[4] See E. R. Franklin, "The Instructions of U. S. Senators by North Carolina," *Historical Papers of the Trinity College Historical Society* (1907).

[5] He was thinking of the New England townships where representation was actually agency or substitution. He was later to move far to the right.

[6] Luce, *Legislative Principles,* pp. 460–77.

1811 and Benton of Missouri in 1848, instructions were disregarded. Reversing the position which he had held during the Senate fight over expunging the Senate censure of Jackson in 1834, Benton declined to accept instructions favoring the admission of slavery in the new states. He claimed that he would appeal to the whole constituency for an opinion on the instructions, and thus postponed the issue until the next election. He was duly defeated.[7]

Most of the time, the practice of instructions met with little opposition. In 1812, however, after Senators Giles and Brent of Virginia had refused to obey the instructions of the legislature, the legislature issued a lengthy resolution upholding instructions.[8] The line of reasoning was as follows:

1. The giving of instructions to representatives had been a legal practice in the House of Commons in England since time immemorial.

2. "Much more unquestionable is it [the right of instructing] in the United States, where the people are acknowledged to be the only legitimate source of all legislation—where the representative and constituent bodies are more intimately connected by the constitution—where none can be a Representative or Senator who shall not, when elected, be an inhabitant of the state for which he is chosen."

3. Citations from authority in America are few but the practice is universally accepted.

4. The nature of representation demands the right of instruction of the representative by the constituents. It is to avoid turbulence and other mischiefs "that representation is substituted for the direct suffrage of these people in the office of legislation. The representative, therefore, must in the nature of things, represent his own particular constituents only. He must, indeed look on the general good of the nation; but he must look also, and especially to the interests of his particular constituents as concerned in the common weal; because the general good is but the aggregate of individual happiness. He must legislate for the whole nation; but laws are expressions of the general will; and the general will is only the result of individual wills farily collected and compared: in order to which collection and comparison [that is, in order to express the general will, in order to make laws] it is plain, that the

---

[7] Theodore Roosevelt, *Thomas Hart Benton* (1887), pp. 342–3.

[8] *Acts of the Commonwealth of Virginia, 1812*, pp. 143–52.

representative must express the will, and speak the opinions, of the constituents that depute him."

5. "It is a maxim of all governments founded on contract, that no man be bound by laws to which he has not given his assent, either directly, or mediately by his representative, or virtually through representatives chosen by his fellow-citizens, amongst whom he dwells, having the same general and local interest with himself."

6. A representative is endowed still with much discretion and confidence, but all of that "is grounded on the supposition, that he is charged with the will, acquainted with the opinions, and devoted to the interests of his constituents."

7. The state legislature is just as much a constituency with regard to the senators as the people are in regard to the representatives.

8. The objection that the sense of the constituency is impossible to ascertain is often true, but when it is proffered as an instruction it cannot be denied.

9. The objection that instructions may be refused because they are unconstitutional may be accepted, but such cases are hard to imagine.

10. The objection that there is no law where there exists no punishment applies only to practice of an evil nature. The highest duties of mankind have no legal sanctions. The acceptance of instructions is one of these duties.

The resolution is most enlightening, even if we admit that political motives were behind the sentiments, for here again a political situation is described in terms of a psychology of the state. Representation is contractual. It is direct. The law of the state is the direct will of the majority. The will of the majority is simply a matter of counting individual wills. Try as he may, the representative cannot escape the fact that society is an aggregate and he is an agent.

T. V. SMITH

Congress Must Follow the Popular Will

T. V. Smith, 1890–1964, taught for two decades at the University of Chicago and then held the chair of Maxwell Professor of Citizenship and Philosophy at Syracuse University. He was a member of both the Illinois Senate (1934–38) and the U.S. House of Representatives (1939–41). He served in both World Wars. Among his books are The Democratic Way of Life (*1939*), The Legislative Way of Life (*1940*), Discipline for Democracy (*1942*), Atomic Power and Moral Faith (*1946*), Abraham Lincoln and the Spiritual Life (*1951*), *and* Man's Threefold Will to Freedom (*1953*).

CONGRESS DOES NOT LEAD. . . . Congress only follows. It is indeed the primary business of Congress to discern and follow the popular will when there is a popular will, and to do nothing where there isn't, save to talk around and about until there is a popular will.

I'm all for Congress as she is, as against her critics; and I am for her following along after the people, instead of getting her out in front to be shot at and to fritter her time away in useless exhortation. What is more, I am convinced that the very people [who say that Congress should lead] don't want Congress to lead. They actually want it to follow: *follow them!* Let Congress get the *lead* on *them*, and you will discern their true intentions by the nocturnal yodeling which then goes up against what has long been called, "The never-ending audacity of elected persons."

Now in these latter complaints, critics of Congress may well be on solider ground. Their complaint is now, note, not against congressional following, but against its following the wrong group

From T. V. Smith, "Should Congress Lead or Follow Public Opinion?", *Town Meeting*, Vol. 8, No. 11 (July 9, 1942), pp. 7–17.

(namely, the *other* group), or following the right group (their group) but at too great a remove. . . .

[Those who would have Congress lead] say, as per Dr. Gallup, for instance . . . "Continuous studies of public opinion show that if majority opinion had been acted upon more often—or more quickly—some of the Nation's present headaches might have been avoided." The [Gallup] article continues with excellent examples to prove—prove what? That Congress should lead? Not at all. Almost the opposite, in fact that Congress should follow majority opinion and follow at its heels. . . .

Let us then look at [the] so-called facts to see what they prove since they do not disprove my thesis that Congress should follow, and since they certainly do not prove . . . that Congress should lead. Take two of [the] complaints that are typical . . . that Congress lags in following public opinion on hours and wages and on lowering the draft age. Now, that's what [one man] thinks, but for whom does [he] speak? Who commissioned [him], or Mr. Gallup, or me to be so oracular on public opinion in a nation of nearly a hundred million citizens?

But somebody did commission a Congressman. Everybody *did* commission Congress to judge as to both the *what* of public opinion and as to the *when* for action under it. Some people and some Congressmen want the draft age lowered. Yes, now; some don't. Some people and some Congressmen wanted hours lengthened and wages stabilized—right then. Some didn't.

Who is to be the judge of the what of public opinion, seldom unambiguous, and who is to pronounce the when where timing is important? Each [interest group] leader, especially if he can command a loud speaker, presumes his group the judge of these questions, but all such groups are unofficial and unauthoritative. Congress alone is official and only Congress is authoritative.

I personally think, for instance, it wise to defer draft lowering until after the election, and the magnificent facts of production themselves already confirm congressional forebearance in letting wages and hours be handled by an acknowledged friend of labor rather than by a segment of Congress inimical to labor.

That's my opinion, you say. Yes, but yours is only yours. Where is ours? Judgment of Congress is ours. It alone is ours. Touching Congress, therefore, I commend with an amendment the returned soldier's advice, "Work like hell and keep your mouth shut." But to amend, "Not too shut."

It's all right to talk [about] and even to criticize your Congress-men if the critic, one, remembers that he's not God and, two, like a good sport accepts whatever it is that Congress actually does. That's the American system—official and authoritative.

This same American system which permits Congress to follow and requires it to compromise . . . provides national leadership also but in other branches of government.

Negatively, leadership is provided by the Supreme Court, which tells Congress what it cannot do. Covertly, it is provided by cab-inet members and more and more in these complex and trying days by important boards and commissions. Conspicuously as well as affirmatively, however, leadership is supplied by the President, who under the Constitution reports to Congress on the state of the nation, and now as a matter of course outlines for Congress what it ought to do. It is respectable for the President thus to lead, and highly effective. It is not respectable for Congress thus to lead. The President . . . will ordinarily be rewarded for aggressive lead-ership by reelection; Congressmen will be penalized for it by defeat. . . . We expect the President to present a program, to fight for it; and, truth to tell, we expect Congress to *follow* him, or another man who will presently supplant him as national leader.

That is one way of doing it. . . . [It] may not be the best way, but it has come to be our American way—and it works rather well. We allow it the defects of its qualities since it has the qualities of its defects.

Hear on this point Abraham Lincoln appealing to his constit-uency for reelection to the General Assembly of Illinois: "If elected," he said, "I shall be governed by their will on all such subjects upon which I have the means of knowing what their will is, and upon all others I shall do what my own judgment teaches me will best advance their interests."

That is a combination of the deputy theory and the representa-tive theory, leaning, as you can see, heavily toward Congress to follow the popular will. Note that ignorance of public opinion is the only loophole Lincoln left himself for any leadership as a legislator. . . .

[A Congressman is bound] by the deepest principle on earth—the principle that the will of the people should prevail as over against any private prejudice, even of the Congressman. . . .

[The voice of the people is the voice of God] until the people change their mind; and then it's the voice of God again, until they change their mind once more. . . .

The deepest conviction that any Congressman in this democracy ever has is that the will of the people ought to prevail. When you think he is selling out other convictions, he is subordinating smaller convictions to the deepest conviction of a democratic representative.

JAMES M. BURNS

Vote for the Important Home Folks First

James MacGregor Burns is James Phinney Baxter Pro-
fessor of History and Public Affairs at Williams College.
He has been active in Massachusetts and national politics
as a member of the Massachusetts delegation to the Demo-
cratic Presidential Convention and as a Democratic can-
didate for Congress. Among his several books are Government by the People (*1951*) (*with Jack Peltason*), Roosevelt: The Lion and the Fox (*1956*), John Kennedy: A
Political Profile (*1960*), *and* The Deadlock of Democracy:
Four Party Politics in America (*1963*). *The following*
selection is Burns' description of what "the biologist would
call a type *genus—the member of Congress who best*
typifies his family. . . . He is a composite of those Sena-
tors and Representatives who year after year and despite
changes in party control determine the make-up of Con-
gress and the main direction it takes." Similarly, the
Ninth District is a typical congressional district and Boone
Center a typical municipality in such a district.

TODAY, IN HIS SIXTH TERM IN THE HOUSE, the Congressman is in
the business of politics, and he is an expert at the trade. He is
honest, shrewd, friendly, unassuming, hard-working. He is exceedingly articulate. He knows how to be prudent and conciliatory
when the situation so demands, and how to be stubborn. He has
a thorough knowledge of the politics and of the business of his
district, and of the ties between politics and business. He has an
acquaintanceship numbered in the thousands. Although he is not
well known outside of his state, the Congressman has been in the

From pp. 4–13 *Congress on Trial* by James M. Burns. Copyright 1949 by Harper & Row,
Publishers, Incorporated.

House long enough to become one of the more influential members. Because he has an increasingly important role in the formation of national policies, the ideas that move him are of concern to all America.

A Credo for Boone Center

The Congressman believes firmly that he is a moderate and a middle-of-the-roader. Although he lays no claim to being even a "little left of center," he has abandoned certain ideas that once dominated his thinking. Fifteen or twenty years ago, for example, he believed that the open shop was the American way—certainly the Boone Center way. Today he champions the labor unions in the city, especially if they are not overly influenced by "outsiders."

He accepts governmental activity in fields today that he would have denounced before the Great Depression: price support for farm products; minimum wage standards for workers; old age pensions. On the other hand, planning, governmental paternalism, and centralized power are repugnant to him. America, he feels, is still the land of opportunity for those with initiative and industry, as Boone Center and the 9th District have been for him.

A section of the preamble to the American Legion constitution sums up his political credo, and he likes to quote it at the climax of his speeches: "To combat the autocracy of both the classes and the masses . . ."

Above all else the Congressman believes in Boone Center and the rest of the 9th District. An unashamed booster of the district, he is an expert on its products, its history, and its importance to the nation. He easily becomes sentimental about the "folks back home," and it is honest sentiment. The ancient question as to whether a member of Congress should act for the nation or for his district bothers him not at all. He simply equates Boone Center's well-being with the national welfare. "The people of the 9th District sent me here to represent their interests first," he often proclaims on the floor of the House, but he sees no real issue on that score.

Next to his district, the Congressman believes in his state and in his country. Disdaining the tactics of those he calls "flag-wavers," he nonetheless feels that more Americanism would help solve the problems facing America. He considers himself a "moderate internationalist," having voted for United States membership in the United Nations. He supports American participation in all international organizations, at the same time demanding that this nation retain her full sovereignty. He opposed the loan to Britain on the grounds that America should not bail out socialist governments, and he believes that loans should be made only to nations maintaining free enterprise systems. He is in favor of lower tariffs, but not for foreign goods competing with products of the 9th District.

Part of his Americanism is a latent hostility toward outsiders. Catholics, Jews, and Negroes form small minorities in his constituency, and the Congressman prides himself on his racial tolerance. Indeed, one of his best friends is a Jew. But there is a decided difference in his mind between racial minorities as individuals and as groups. He conceives of minority peoples, especially those in the great urban areas, as tending to harbor alien and un-American ideas. He feels that the amount of racial and religious discrimination in this country is exaggerated, and that the best way to handle the slight intolerance that exists is to ignore it. Making an issue of discrimination simply aggravates it. Incitement to racial and class feeling he vigorously opposes.

Considering that vote-getting is his trade, the Congressman has a curiously ambivalent attitude toward politics and parties. As a practical politician he knows that the daily negotiations and give-and-take are central to the democratic process. Yet he feels that some of the great issues of the day, such as foreign policy, should be kept out of the arena of political conflict. "Politics stops at the water's edge," is a favorite slogan of his.

He is especially critical of party politics in this respect. His own partisanship is a matter of form and little content. Boone Center people are Republican or Democratic nationally, but party ties bind them loosely in local affairs, and the congressional election is considered a matter of local concern. Sane and stable government is possible only if both parties follow a middle-of-the-road course, he believes, and nothing would be worse than a labor party arrayed against a party of business. Although Boone Center has an elaborate class system, he would hate to see politics conducted along class lines.

The Congressman is flatly against "big government." The huge bureaucracy he often pictures as an octopus seated in Washington with its tentacles reaching into every corner of the land. Knowing the many services rendered his constituents, he defends the work of a number of the bureaus, but he looks forward to the day when the trend toward more central government can be reversed. Just how the reversal is to be accomplished he is not sure.

The Congressman distrusts the bureaucrats as a group. They are experts in their fields, while he must be a political jack-of-all-trades. They are theorists and technicians, while he would like to see more "practical" people in government, like himself. Worst of all, they exercise power without having earned the right to do so, he feels. He complains that none of them "could get elected dog catcher" in his home town.

"I am fearful of these experts," he once said on the floor of the House. "The brain trust has cost us money every time it went into action. In my opinion, it will take some farmers from county seats to do the job."

The Congressman is not a man of political principle. He spurns the national platform of his party because it contains provisions designed to appease or attract groups throughout the country in whom he has no interest. But he has no real substitute of his own for such a platform. He has only a bundle of symbols and a sheaf of special claims for Boone Center's organized interests. He believes in Americanism, Democracy, Justice, Freedom, and Patriotism, and he knows why Boone Center needs a new postoffice and why its industries should have more tariff protection and why World War II veterans should have a bonus.

But between the misty symbol and the special plea he takes no stand on the vital national issues on which the presidential elections are at least in part fought out—on taxes and spending, on housing and river development, on full employment and fair employment, on relief and reconstruction abroad, on health and social security. He is no broker of ideas. Indeed, one of his most effective vote-winning techniques is to evade taking positions on thorny problems in order not to alienate voters.

How the Congressman steers clear of matters of policy and principle and sails calm political waters as diplomatic agent of the 9th District in Washington offers at once a clue to the Congressman's tenacity in office and a lesson in American political mechanics.

Diplomatic Agent

Though he may not admit it even to himself, the Congressman's chief aim is re-election. To stay in office means to gain added power and prerogatives in Congress on the basis of seniority, and to become eligible ultimately for higher office—senator, governor, judge, cabinet member. If his re-election depended on successful exploitation of key national issues, the Congressman would be compelled to run on the record of his votes on those issues. But his success at the polls hinges largely on how effectively the Congressman has served as the 9th District's representative in Washington. Here his record is almost flawless. He has rarely faltered in his protection of the sovereign interests of his locality. Against the encroachments of Big Business, Big Labor, and Big Government he has defended the rights of small business, local unions, and the average man in his district. By seeming to protect the totality of the 9th District's interests against the outside world, the Congressman contrives to avoid the basic but perilous issues of national and world policy.

But if the Congressman has little responsibility to his constituents on matters of broad public policy, he has a very definite responsibility to two groups in the 9th District. One of these consists of the local party leaders—called "bosses" by their opponents —and the other of the organized special interest groups.

The party bosses in the 9th District are concerned almost wholly with patronage and favors. They are not evil or venal men; they know that without patronage their political dominion, centered in city, courthouse, and county machines, would soon crumble. Operating at all levels of American government, they extract from Washington jobs for their followers as postmasters, federal marshals, collectors of internal revenue, judges, and the like. In state and local governments an army of petty officials makes obeisance to the machine for its jobs.

The Congressman advanced smoothly up the ladder from assistant county attorney to his present position only because he never failed to cooperate with his party leaders on matters of patronage. He is fully aware that he needs their support more than they need his supply of federal patronage. For in the case of falling-out and a showdown—an unthinkable occurrence for the Congressman—he could cut off only one source of their patronage; the bosses would survive to put an end to his political career in the next party primary, over which they exercise a tight grip.

The local party leaders, for the most part, have little interest in the Congressman's votes on national issues. Even when he deserts the national party platform on important legislation, it never occurs to the party leaders that they have any responsibility for that platform. Indeed, the party machine itself often has a bi-partisan slant because of unwritten covenants with the other major party over matters of patronage.

In several cases, however, the local leaders are concerned as individuals, rather than as party officials, with the Congressman's position on certain national policies. A leader of one of Boone Center's wards, for example, is a large lumber dealer, and naturally he is interested in the Congressman's votes on such matters as price control, housing, and subsidies. Two of the county leaders operate large farms and have considerable influence in the Grange; they follow the Congressman's votes on farm bills with care.

The other dominant element in the 9th District—the cluster of organized interest groups—has no concern with patronage but a deep concern with national legislation. The most important pressure groups in the district are those of business, farmers, veterans, and labor, in that order. These groups in turn are made up of individual organizations. The farmers, for example, are divided into the National Grange, the American Farm Bureau Federation, the National Cooperative Milk Producers' Federation, and the Farmers' Union. The veterans divide into the American Legion, the Veterans of Foreign Wars, and World War II organizations. Special issue groups, such as Townsendites and Prohibitionists, take an active part in politics. And there are scores of fraternal, religious, national-origin, and occupational associations.

How many votes do these groups control? The Congressman wishes he knew the answer to this question. With a sharp eye for political margins, he perceives that some organizations lay claim to large membership, like-minded on all issues, where actually the rank-and-file is small in number, divided, and irresolute. But he cannot be sure. He must feel his way cautiously. Whether or not the pressure groups deliver the votes, they are important media of communication with thousands of voters. The political apathy in his district is often so great that he is unable to "get to" the electorate. The various associations, with their meetings, newspapers, and radio programs, can help him make connections with many voters who might never attend a party rally or read ordinary campaign literature.

Naturally the Congressman tries to gauge the reality of vote-power behind the facade of propaganda. But his responsiveness to the pressure groups is not a matter of votes alone. Often the Congressman makes political decisions without any evaluation of the exact line-up of the various groups back home. He truly "votes

his own conscience." If his position happens to coincide with that
of the organized groups in his district, it is not simply because he
is controlled by them. It is because he is one of them. He is a
Legionnaire; he is close to the farmers and their interests; his roots
are in the business class. He knows the leaders of the various
organizations, and by and large he considers them "sound."

Even the Congressman, with all his political dexterity, cannot
act for every one of the groups. To some extent he must choose
sides. In practice he speaks for a coalition of groups representing
small business, the owners of large farms, veterans of three wars,
and skilled labor. He speaks for these groups partly because they
are politically effective, partly because he lives in their political
world. Thus the business organizations, the Grange, the Farm
Bureau, the Legion, the VFW, and the American Federation of
Labor carry weight in the congressional representation of the 9th
District.

Since even these interests may come into conflict, the Congressman must be able to act for one of them without seeming to flout
the claims of the others. Consequently, he moves quickly to confer
legislative favors on one pressure group where he can do so without injuring another. He selects his ground carefully. A bonus for
veterans, subsidies and price support for farmers, high tariffs for
business, the prevailing wage for AFL crafts—such measures are
well adapted to the Congressman's use, for not one of them is
likely to antagonize the other groups. Tariff protection for the
small industries of the 9th District is an especially effective campaign argument because it appeals to both business and labor.
Higher farm prices are justified as leading to more spending by
farmers in Boone Center's shops. Such measures may mean a
higher cost of living for the consumers of the 9th District, but consumers do not make up one of the pressure groups that the Congressman must reckon with on election day.

The Congressman reflects a sense of solidarity in the 9th District
that is not wholly artificial. Not only Boone Center but the whole
district is essentially a trading and producing community. The
operators of big farms, employing machinery and hired hands,
must be businessmen as well as farmers. On the local scale there
is little disharmony between them and the businessmen of the city.
The traders in Boone Center, who were originally independent and
self-contained, during the past half-century have increasingly become instruments of a nation-wide commercial system. At one

time free agents, Boone Center factories are now units of a national industrial order. But the myth of the autonomous and footloose community still persists, and the Congressman loses few votes in the 9th District when he attacks Wall Street and Big Business. For the dominant forces in both city and country have been steeped in the ideas of a local pecuniary society operating on its own. Militantly conservative, the substantial citizens of the district produce on the local level a gloss which partially coneals latent conflicts between large and small business, between business and industry, between workers and employer, between farm owner and hired hand, between city and country, between producer and consumer.

The most serious threat to the Congressman's strategy lies in the dramatization of epochal national questions such as often dominate the political scene during presidential campaigns. The exploitation of key issues by a Roosevelt or a Willkie, by a Wallace or a Stassen, draws unorganized voters to the polls and disrupts the united fronts assumed by pressure groups around their narrow designs. Such issues induce members of even the most tightly organized groups to forsake their petty interests and to think and vote in terms of broad national policy.

In such a juncture the Congressman assumes the politician's protective coloration—he straddles. Refusing to accept the gauge of battle on the open ground of national policy, he retires into a defensive zone of evasion, subterfuge, and recourse to "red herrings." At all costs he shifts the debate away from his position on controversial public policy and focusses attention on his fight for the 9th District and its interests. Here he is on safe ground.

Against the injection of national issues into the local campaign the Congressman's best defense is the absence of a clear-cut record on those issues. On some important votes in the House there was no record as to how the members lined up. The Congressman was not obliged to take a position on some matters because the bills died in the Senate or in committee. When other bills came before the House he may have been unavoidably detained on business in his office or district, and thus unable to vote.

The most effective way to straddle an issue, he has discovered, is to vote on both sides of the question. On one occasion the Congressman voted to kill a bill by recommitting it; half an hour after the recommittal move, he cast his ballot for the legislation. In the case of the price control act of 1942 he advocated a series of crippling amendments, some of which favored manufacturers and farmers in the 9th District, but in the end he voted for the Act. On several occasions he supported measures in Congress only to take part later in "economy drives" that would have starved the agency enforcing the laws. These subterfuges have obvious advantages. In case he is questioned back home as to his stand on these policies, the Congressman can tailor his answer to fit the views of his inquirers and he can point to the record to back up his claims.

If the Congressman were a modern Machiavelli, his advice to freshmen in Congress on "How to Stay in Office" would be: (1) vote for the home folks first, especially for those who are well organized; (2) keep on good terms with the local party bosses; (3) stress your protection of your district's interests as a whole against the outside world; (4) as far as possible do not commit yourself on the important national issues that divide your constituents. But the Congressman is not Machiavellian, and if he gave such advice he would speak in terms of the importance of following a safe and sane middle way, of the dangers of extremism and centralization, of the need for protecting local rights and interests.

HADLEY CANTRIL

The People Prefer Delegates

Hadley Cantril, formerly a professor of psychology at Harvard, has served as Director of a UNESCO project on world tensions, and is the author of The Psychology of Social Movements (*1941*), Understanding Man's Social Behavior (*1947*), The Why of Man's Experience (*1950*) *and* Human Nature and Political Systems (*1961*). *He also edited the volume* Public Opinion, 1935–1946 *from which the following poll is taken.*

US Nov '38: Do you believe that a Congressman should vote on any question as the majority of his constituents desire or vote according to his own judgments? (FOR)[1] *Aug 8 '39 and Apr 17 '40:* Should Members of Congress vote according to their own best judgment or according to the way the people in their districts feel? *Apr 18 '40:* In cases when a Congressman's opinion is different from that of the majority of the people in his district, do you think he should usually vote according to his own best judgment, or according to the way the majority of his district feels? (AIPO)[2]

	Way people feel	*Own judgment*	*No opinion or Don't know*
Nov '38	37.4%	54.1%	8.5% = 100%
Aug 8 '39	61	39 = 100%	4
Apr 17 '40	66	34 = 100	6
Apr 18 '40	63	37 = 100	8

[1] *Fortune* magazine [Editor's note].

[2] American Institute of Public Opinion (Gallup) [Editor's note].

From Hadley Cantril and O. Strunk, *Public Opinion 1935–1946* (Princeton, 1951), p. 133. Reprinted by permission of Princeton University Press.

HENRY A. WALLACE

Vote With the Party on Key Issues

Henry Agard Wallace, 1888–1965, was an editor, farm businessman, administrator, and politician. Originally a Republican, he served as F. D. R.'s Secretary of Agriculture (1933–1940) and as Vice President (1941–1945). He resigned as Secretary of Commerce in the first Truman administration to edit the New Republic *and then to campaign for the Presidency in 1948 on the Progressive party ticket. In 1950 he left the Progressive party after it repudiated his endorsement of the US-UN police action in Korea. His books include* America Must Choose *(1934),* The Century of the Common Man *(1943), and* Sixty Million Jobs *(1945).*

IT IS UNDOUBTEDLY TRUE that we have become somewhat cynical about party platforms and that, all too often, we have been complacent when our representatives and senators failed to support even the major policies of their party. Moreover, I have heard more than one man prominent in public life remark that only a politically naïve person would expect a congressman to support the promises in his party's platform.

I do not believe, however, that the American people are as completely cynical as this. I am certain that today the people are showing more concern over the actions of their elected representatives

From Henry A. Wallace, "Party Responsibility," *Collier's Magazine* (June 22, 1946).

than at any time since the formation of our Republic. I believe that most citizens agree that we must find a way to make the people's representatives responsible for their actions—responsible to those who listen to their promises and elect them on the basis of those promises. . . .

Those back home who voted for Democratic congressmen have been dismayed at finding too many of them voting against Democratic legislation. Republicans have been equally dismayed to find Republicans voting for Democratic legislation. [A Republican leader in the Senate once] . . . expressed deep concern over the confusion in voting among Republican congressmen. He said that to elect New Dealers as Republican congressmen would "only confound the present confusion and . . . betray those who entrust the future to Republican leadership.

Thus, it is not only the Democratic side that is concerned over party responsibility. Indeed, this is a problem that must concern everyone, since it involves our most cherished institution—representative government. . . .

I am writing this article not only to expand my own views, but also in the hope that it will bring forth the ideas of others so that the nation can have a beneficial debate on this vital subject. And I am dealing specifically with what should be done by the elected party. To this end, I want to present the following beliefs:

I believe that delegates should determine at a party's national convention certain major policies their candidates will go all out to support for the next four years. This platform should be drawn up —with all seriousness and after full democratic deliberation—in the knowledge that the citizens of the United States will hold the party accountable for its platform promises.

When the new Congress is organized, the leaders of the majority party in both houses—in consultation with the President and his Cabinet—should immediately select from the platform several planks that, in their opinion, concern the most important problems facing the nation. These planks would then become the test issues for determining party responsibility and party loyalty. . . .

In making the selections, the majority party leaders of the House and Senate should discuss party policy thoroughly with the party's representatives and senators before deciding on the test issues. For this purpose, I believe most strongly that party caucuses should be held more often. . . .

Once the basic test policies of the majority party have been selected, the congressmen of that party would be required to vote with the party on bills designed to put these policies into action. But they would not have to vote with the party leadership on other party measures.

But who and what will require them to vote with the party? And what is to prevent the people from returning them to Congress in spite of their failure to live up to the party's platform promises? Here are some of the answers:

The party organization in Congress could deprive a dissident congressman of his most valuable privileges. The first result of disloyalty to party principles could be the loss of membership in Congressional committees. The dissenting congressman would still have his democratic right to speak and vote on the floor, but he could not participate in the highly important legislative decisions that are made in committee before bills reach the floor.

The constituents of a congressman without committee privileges would not long return him to Congress.

Dissident representatives or senators could also be deprived of their privilege of influencing appointments to federal offices. These appointments usually are subject to review by the National Committee of the party in power, which could discipline a congressman by completely ignoring his recommendations.

On first thought, this may seem like harsh discipline. But the demands of our time—the demands upon our democratic system—also are harsh. And we shall never have a healthy two-party system as long as a recalcitrant minority of the party in power fattens itself on party patronage and committee seniority and still flouts the party leadership that seeks to carry out a people's mandate.

Even if a congressman had shown himself a party man in name but not in deed, he would still be free to seek renomination under the party label in his own state primary or convention. If such a dissident congressman were reelected and then followed the party leadership on the test issues, party privileges would be restored to him.

I do not advocate, nor do I believe in, the direct use of the national party machinery against a dissident congressman in his own state. I was opposed to the so-called "purge" of 1938—and I told President Roosevelt so on three different occasions. However, I do believe that the President and other party leaders have the obligation to make their views known about dissident congressmen so that the voters can be fully informed. But the direct use of the national party machinery against dissidents in their own states would be an undemocratic act interfering with the people's right to choose their own representatives in free elections. . . .

In outlining my proposal, I have not attempted to answer all possible objections as I went along. I well know, however, that all manner of sincere questions will arise and I shall try to anticipate some of them.

Someone is sure to ask: "With this kind of party discipline, wouldn't a senator or representative be merely a rubber stamp?" The answer is that no congressman, as I have said, would be asked to follow the party leadership on every measure. He would be required to vote with the party only on those few basic issues that party leaders, after full consultation, decided were vital to the general welfare, from the party's own point of view.

Suppose a congressman followed the party leadership on some measure against his own better judgment. He would be at perfect liberty to go back to the voters at home and tell them frankly that he voted against his own wishes, that he personally was opposed to the party policy on this particular measure, and that he would work unceasingly to change this party policy. Such activities should not be cause for imposing disciplinary action.

Others will ask: "If issues develop after the platforms have been voted on by the people, will the new issues be made a test of party loyalty?" The answer is: "Yes, if they are basic to the party's position." For example, no one could have predicted, in the summer of 1944, that the control and utilization of atomic energy would become one of the most important issues before the present Congress. Certainly, the peacetime development of atomic energy should be a basic issue for testing party loyalty and party responsibility. . . .

Another question that may be asked is: "What can the people do about party platforms besides voting for or against the platforms presented to them at election time?" The people can have a great deal to say about the platforms of their parties if they become active in politics at the precinct level—and keep active.

All too often in the past we have become excited along about the end of October—only to become complacent again after the first week in November. The challenge to democracy today cannot be met by this kind of dabbling in politics.

Their national interest demands that the people constantly exercise their privileges of citizenship right down to the precinct level.

If they do this, they will find that they have a powerful voice in the selection of delegates to party conventions and, through these delegates, in making party platforms. . . .

In the decisive days ahead, the American people have definite alternatives ahead of them.

They can make an effective and intelligent choice only if our political parties stand openly and honestly for clearly defined principles—and can be counted upon to put those principles into action when the people have made their decision.

A. P. S. A. COMMITTEE ON POLITICAL PARTIES

We Need a More Responsible Two-Party System

The following selection is taken from the 1950 report of the Committee on Political Parties of the American Political Science Association. This Committee consisted of E. E. Schattschneider, Thomas S. Barclay, Clarence A. Berdahl, Hugh A. Bone, Franklin L. Burdette, Paul T. David, Merle Fainsod, Bertram M. Gross, E. Allen Helms, E. M. Kirkpatrick, John W. Lederle, Fritz Morstein Marx, Louise Overacker, Howard Penniman, Kirk H. Porter, and J. B. Shannon.

The Role of the Political Parties

The Parties and Public Policy. Popular government in a nation of more than 150 million people requires political parties which provide the electorate with a proper range of choice between alternatives of action. In order to keep the parties apart, one must consider the relations between each and public policy. The reasons for the growing emphasis on public policy in party politics are to be found, above all, in the very operations of modern government.

The New Importance of Program. The crux of public affairs lies in the necessity for more effective formulation of general policies and programs and for better integration of all of the far-flung activities of modern government. It is in terms of party programs that political leaders can attempt to consolidate public attitudes toward the work plans of government.

The Potentialities of the Party System. The potentialities of the two-party system are suggested, on the one hand, by the fact that for all practical purposes the major parties monopolize elections; and,

From "Toward a More Responsible Two-Party System," *The American Political Science Review,* Vol. XLIV, No. 3 (September, 1950), pp. 1–3, 7, 8, 10. Reprinted by permission of The American Political Science Association.

on the other, by the fact that both parties have in the past managed to adapt themselves to the demands made upon them by external necessities. It is good practical politics to reconsider party organization in the light of the changing conditions of politics. Happily such an effort entails an application of ideas about the party system that are no longer unfamiliar.

What Kind of Party System Is Needed?

The party system that is needed must be democratic, responsible and effective.

A STRONGER TWO-PARTY SYSTEM

The Need for an Effective Party System. An effective party system requires, first, that the parties are able to bring forth programs to which they commit themselves and, second, that the parties possess sufficient internal cohesion to carry out these programs. Such a degree of unity within the parties cannot be brought about without party procedures that give a large body of people an opportunity to share in the development of the party program.

The Need for an Effective Opposition Party. The fundamental requirement of accountability is a two-party system in which the opposition party acts as the critic of the party in power, developing, defining and presenting the policy alternatives which are necessary for a true choice in reaching public decisions. The opposition most conducive to responsible government is an organized party opposition.

BETTER INTEGRATED PARTIES

The Need for a Party System with Greater Resistance to Pressure. There is little to suggest that the phenomenal growth of interest organizations in recent decades has come to its end. The whole development makes necessary a reinforced party system that can cope with the multiplied organized pressures. Compromise among interests is compatible with the aims of a free society only when the terms of reference reflect an openly acknowledged concept of the public interest.

The Need for a Party System with Sufficient Party Loyalty. Needed clarification of party policy will not cause the parties to differ more fundamentally or more sharply than they have in the past. Nor is it to be assumed that increasing concern with their programs will cause the parties to erect between themselves an ideological wall. Parties have the right and the duty to announce the terms to govern participation in the common enterprise. The emphasis in all consideration of party discipline must be on positive measures to create a strong and general agreement on policies. A basis for party cohesion in Congress will be established as soon as the parties interest themselves sufficiently in their congressional candidates to set up strong and active campaign organizations in the constituencies.

MORE RESPONSIBLE PARTIES

The Need for Parties Responsible to the Public. Party responsibility means the responsibility of both parties to the general public, as enforced in elections. Party responsibility to the public, enforced in elections, implies that there be more than one party, for the public can hold a party responsible only if it has a choice. As a means of achieving responsibility, the clarification of party policy also tends to keep public debate on a more realistic level, restraining the inclination of party spokesmen to make unsubstantiated statements and charges.

The Need for Parties Responsible to Their Members. Party responsibility includes also the responsibility of party leaders to the party membership, as enforced in primaries, caucuses and conventions. The external and the internal kinds of party responsibility need not conflict. Intraparty conflict will be minimized if it is generally recognized that national, state and local party leaders have a common responsibility to the party membership. National party leaders have a legitimate interest in the nomination of congressional candidates. . . .

Party Platforms. Alternatives between the parties are defined so badly that it is often difficult to determine what the election has decided even in broadest terms. The prevailing procedure for the writing and adoption of national party platforms is too hurried and too remote from the process by which actual decisions are made to command the respect of the whole party and the electorate. The platform should be the end product of a long search for a working agreement within the party. . . .

Binding Character. In spite of clear implications and express pledges, there has been much difference of opinion as to the exact binding quality of a platform. All of this suggests the need for appropriate machinery, such as a Party Council, to interpret and apply the national program in respect to doubts or details. When that is done by way of authoritative and continuing statement, the party program should be considered generally binding. . . .

Caucuses or Conferences. More frequent meetings of the party membership in each house should be held. A binding caucus decision on legislative policy should be used primarily to carry out the party's principles and programs. When members of Congress disregard a caucus decision taken in furtherance of national party policy, they should expect disapproval. The party leadership committees should be responsible for calling more frequent caucuses or conferences and developing the agenda of points for discussion. . . .

Toward a New Concept of Party Membership. The existence of a national program, drafted at frequent intervals by a party convention both broadly representative and enjoying prestige, should make a great difference. It would prompt those who identify themselves as Republicans or Democrats to think in terms of support of that program, rather than in terms of personalities, patronage and local matters. Once machinery is established which gives the party member and his representative a share in framing the party's objectives, once there are safeguards against internal dictation by a few in positions of influence, members and representatives will feel readier to assume an obligation to support the program. Membership defined in these terms does not ask for mindless discipline enforced from above. It generates self-discipline which stems from free identification with aims one helps to define.

JULIUS TURNER

Party Pressure Is Significant in Congress

Julius Turner, 1922–1952, was one of the most promising young scholars in the field of American politics at the time of his death at age thirty. He received his Ph.D. from Johns Hopkins in 1950 and taught there, at Boston University, and at Allegheny College where he held the rank of Associate Professor. The Julius Turner Award, given annually at Johns Hopkins University for the most outstanding essay in Political Science, commemorates his work as teacher and scholar.

THE STUDY OF THE EFFECTIVENESS of party pressure on congressional votes is most significant when the results are applied to current controversies over party reform. There is a strong modern movement among political scientists towards reform of the party system along lines that will make the parties less similar and better disciplined—more amenable, in other words, to party pressure. This movement is countered by a less vocal but perhaps more powerful group which maintains that the party system is satisfactory, and that tampering with the present alignment might be dangerous.

The participants in the modern discussion of party responsibility have not seen fit to conduct systematic investigation of the number and kinds of issues on which party pressure is successfully brought to bear on congressmen. Such investigation has appeared unnecessary because the major disputants have been in general agreement as to the existing facts. The proponents of reform as well as those who advocate the status quo have concluded that under the present system the parties do not unite behind distinctly differentiated

From Julius Turner, *Party and Constituency: Pressures on Congress* (Baltimore, 1951), pp. 22–23, 29–33, 165–166. Copyright 1952, The Johns Hopkins Press. Reprinted by permission of the Johns Hopkins Press.

programs. A quantitative study of party pressure might be considered unnecessary, in view of the agreement of most political scientists that party discipline is ineffective today, if it were not for the small voice of a few politicians and at least one historian[1] who claim that significant party differences exist.

RESULTS OF ROLL CALL ANALYSIS

Quantitative analysis of roll call votes shows, contrary to majority opinion, that significant differences exist between our major parties. While it is true that American discipline falls short of that achieved in some European democracies, and is less effective than party discipline in the McKinley era in the United States, evidence of great party influence can still be found. Party pressure seems to be more effective than any other pressure on congressional voting, and is discernible on nearly nine-tenths of the roll calls examined. . . .

FREQUENCY OF SIGNIFICANT PARTY DISAGREEMENT

In view of the contrast between the amount of party voting in the modern American Congress and in Great Britain and France, the question might be asked whether there is any significance, as far as roll call behavior is concerned, in American party membership. The answer to this question, based on statistical testing, is "Yes, party was a significant factor on almost 90 per cent of the roll calls in the modern sessions studied."

Determination of party differences on roll calls requires an objective and sensitive test. When parties are unanimous, or nearly unanimous, in opposition to each other on a roll call, it is easy to find a difference between the attitudes of the parties on the issue. When, however, insurgents within each party cross party lines to vote with the opposition, it becomes more difficult to determine whether party affiliation was connected in any way with the votes cast.

Consider a typical example, the final vote on the salary publicity act repealer of 1937. On this roll call Republicans voted 66 "yea," 11 "nay"; and Democrats 168 "yea," 93 "nay." The immediate observation in this case would be that a majority of both parties favored the repealer, although there were insurgents on both sides. Closer scrutiny reveals that the Republicans were much more favor-

---

[1] See Wilfred E. Binkley. *President and Congress* (New York, 1947), p. vii. Professor Binkley concludes that Republicans and Democrats have differed consistently on the powers of the President and Congress.

able to repeal than were the Democrats. Republicans favored it by more than six to one; Democrats by less than two to one.

Now the question arises whether the difference between the proportions favoring the repealer in the two parties was sufficient so that we may conclude that party pressure had something to do with the result. Obviously, if Democrats favored a measure 100 to 25, and Republicans 99 to 26, we could hardly say that the Democrats were significantly more favorable to the bill. The chance mistake of one Democrat or one Republican in gathering information or in casting his vote might have caused the difference, as could the chance absence of members because of sickness or other factors not connected with party affiliation. If, on the other hand, the Democratic vote were divided 120 to 5, and the Republican 5 to 120, most observers would be willing to concede the influence of party. Somewhere between these extreme examples lies the point where our deduction that party affiliation caused the observed voting behavior passes from the implausible to the plausible.

A usual method employed by statisticians to determine whether the behavior of two groups is significantly dissimilar is to determine the probability that the observed behavior could occur if the two groups had been selected by chance. If, from a glass bowl containing the names and votes on a roll call of 250 congressmen, we should select at random 125 men and call them Democrats, and 125 whom we would call Republicans, what chance would there be that the voting behavior of these synthetic parties would differ to the extent found in the actual roll call vote? The chances that they would disagree in proportions as great as 5 to 120 and 120 to 5 are extremely slim. The chances are much greater that the proportions of "yea" votes in the two synthetic parties would be similar.

A customary statistical level for separating significant group behavior from the doubtful or insignificant is one chance in one hundred; that is, those roll calls may be judged significant in terms of party on which the chances were less than one in a hundred that the parties would differ to that extent if their membership was selected by chance. The method used to determine the probability that the observed division would occur is the chi-square test.

Table 1 shows the number and proportion of roll calls in each of the eight relatively modern sessions studied, on which the behavior of the two parties was sufficiently dissimilar so that there was less than one chance in a hundred that such dissimilarity was due to chance factors.

TABLE 1

AMERICAN PARTY DIFFERENCES: PROPORTION OF ROLL CALL
ON WHICH REPUBLICAN AND DEMOCRATIC BEHAVIOR
DIFFERED SIGNIFICANTLY, EIGHT SESSIONS

| Year | Total Number of Roll Calls | Roll Calls on which Party Differences Significant[a] | |
		Number	Per Cent
1921	56	48	85.7
1928	42	37	88.1
1930-31	29	24	82.8
1933	40	36	90.0
1937	85	74	87.1
1944	56	48	85.7
1945	80	76	95.0
1948	67	64	95.5
Total	455	407	89.5

[a] As measured by the chi-square test. P equals 1/100.

Nearly 90 per cent of the roll calls in the four sessions, 407 of
the 455 votes, divided the parties to an extent sufficient so that the
differences between the parties could be termed significant. Such
behavior occurred with about the same frequency in each of the
eight sessions. On over 17 out of every 20 roll calls studied there was
a significant relationship between party membership and voting
behavior.

The High Degree of Party Loyalty. The telling effect of party
pressure can be seen, furthermore, in the large number of times
that party members voted with the majority of their own party
when the majority of the other party voted on the other side of the
question. As shown in Table 2, of 4658 major party members in
the House in eleven recent sessions studied, only 181, or less than
4 per cent, voted more often with the opposition party than with
their own. The greatest amount of insurgency occurred in 1946, in
President Truman's first year in office. The percentage in that year,
14.3, was much higher than in the other sessions studied. In subsequent sessions, however, the proportion of bolters has dropped
to customary levels.

Even those few representatives who voted more often with their
opponents, however, are important to an understanding of the

TABLE 2

AMERICAN PARTY UNITY: PROPORTION OF HOUSE MEMBERS WHO VOTED WITH THE OPPOSITION MORE OFTEN THAN WITH THEIR OWN PARTY, ELEVEN MODERN SESSIONS

Year	Number of Members[a]	Voted More Often with Opposition	
		Number	Per Cent
1921	423	3	0.7
1928	423	12	2.8
1930-31	419	21	5.0
1933	428	7	1.6
1937	412	8	1.9
1944	425	17	4.0
1946	428	61	14.3
1947	421	3	0.7
1948	424	1	0.2
1949	425	25	5.9
1950	430	23	5.3
Total	4658	181	3.9

[a] Includes only Republicans and Democrats who voted on one-third or more of the roll calls on which the parties were opposed.

American party system. Apparently a man can remain within a party, and be elected to office to represent it, even when on a majority of the issues brought to a record vote in Congress he prefers the position taken by the opposition. Party membership, as far as some representatives are concerned, appears to be based on a qualitative, rather than a quantitative analysis of the issues dividing the parties. A representative who differs more than half the time with his party colleagues may possibly retain his party allegiance because he believes the issues on which he agrees with his party to be of particular importance. There were two Wisconsin Republicans in 1931, nevertheless, who differed with their party on every single issue on which their party disagreed with the Democrats. Both listed themselves in the *Congressional Directory* as Republicans, although they subsequently ran for Congress as Progressives.

Behavior on roll call votes in Congress, therefore, may in some cases have nothing whatsoever to do with the party affiliation of the member, although in the great majority of cases party members show a high degree of similarity in their votes. . . .

Representative Government Through the House of Representatives

The effective coordination of representative government with democratic ideology provokes, perhaps necessarily, some contradictions which confuse our understanding of the American governmental system. Americans set forth as a principal demand upon their legislators that they be "independent" in their actions in government. The candidate is rash who will not announce that he is "fearless," that he has made "no promises to special groups," that he will "follow the President when he is right," but will remain free to "vote his convictions." American political mythology is crammed with the sagas of representatives who defied the demands of party and constituency in order to do what the representative believed to be right.

Against this goal of representative independence Americans set up the conflicting goal of representative responsibility. We demand that our rulers periodically return to be judged by the electorate as to the wisdom of their actions in office. While the independence of the representative may bring him support in the election from some of his constituents, he will find, if he has been "fearless" in his actions, that his independence has cost him the support of groups important to his re-election. He has failed to support farm parity: his district's farmers will not vote for him. The appropriations have been cut for the naval base in his district: the shipworkers will not vote for him and the owners are contributing to his opponent's campaign. He bolted his party on five measures which the President wanted passed for the national campaign: national party leaders are sending speakers and money to help his opponent in the primary, and the vacant postmastership in the representative's home town has been filled without his knowledge by a man he does not know.

The conflict between the ideal of independence and the reality of the demand for responsibility has resulted in a curious situation. The ideal of independence is often upheld by representatives in their speeches, and perhaps in their unrecorded activities in government, but their responsibility to the groups which can bring about their election is maintained in the votes of the great majority of congressmen. The number of congressmen is very small who over a large number of roll calls can successfully resist the pressures of constituency and party. And those who do resist these pressures are eliminated from office more quickly than other representatives.

Of course there are many congressmen who are caught between conflicting pressures, whose party and constituency, or whose groups within the constituency, disagree as to what the congressman should do. Such congressmen are beset with a greater problem than those whose party and all constituent groups urge them to vote for the same legislation. Representatives subject to conflicting pressures must be able to balance these pressures, decide which ones are more important, or attempt to please all by casting conflicting votes on a succession of roll calls. In some cases, on the other hand, a congressman with conflicting pressures may be more free than others to exercise independent judgment. If any move he makes is likely to arouse both support and opposition, he may be able to depend to a greater extent on his own feelings in the matter.

The extent to which congressmen follow the pressures of party and some of the pressures of the constituency (metropolitan-rural, foreign-native, and section) has been shown. . . . Each of these pressures has been shown to be important on some issues in both parties in all years studied, although the pressure of party was much more important than any of the constituent pressures. Even in the case of party, however, we have found at least a few men on almost every roll call who have ignored party pressure and voted with the other party. This revolt on the part of some congressmen against the pressure of party might be termed "independence." In many cases, however, we discover that when a representative bolts his party he is not voting his conscience, but answering the more insistent pressure of groups in his constituency which disagree with the party. A very large number of congressional votes, therefore, may be accounted for as reflections of the pressure of either party or constituency. . . .

CONCLUSION

One central conclusion is to be drawn . . . on congressional voting behavior. That conclusion is that the representative process as practised in twentieth-century America involves, insofar as voting behavior is concerned, the attempt of the representative to mirror the political desires of those groups which can bring about his election or defeat. There are, to be sure, a few representatives who ignore political pressure and go down to defeat, and there are a few others who are fortunate to represent districts where the electoral process is not sufficiently developed for pressure groups and parties to arrange reprisals at the polls. The great majority of congressmen, nevertheless, yield to the pressures from their constituencies, and especially to the pressures of party, in casting their votes. This picture of American representative government may not perhaps conform to the ideal of good government which some men may propose. The American Congress, is, nevertheless, a mirror of political pressure.

THE REPRESENTATIVE AS POLITICO

ROBERT LUCE

The Lawmaker Must be Both Agent and Trustee

Robert Luce, 1862–1946, served in the Massachusetts legislature, as Lieutenant Governor of Massachusetts, and as a member of Congress between 1919 and 1927. He authored a number of books on legislative bodies including Legislative Procedure (*1922*), Legislative Assemblies (*1924*), Legislative Principles (*1930*), *and* Legislative Problems (*1935*).

PUBLIC OPINION [is] the source of legislation. . . . It is not true, however, that the legislator plays or should play no constructive part. He must lead as well as follow. The paradox is explained if you consider that public opinion is often vague, unformed, perhaps hardly more than an instinct. The legislator has the duty of enlightening and guiding, forming and formulating. This it is that justifies him in constructive thought. Were it otherwise, he need never concern himself with more than trying to determine what people want. Limited to a matter of interpretation, the task would never attract men of originality and genius. The race of statesmen would disappear. It will be a sad day when representatives are forbidden to think of what the people ought to want, a sad day when leadership becomes an offence. A citizen does not cease to be a citizen upon election to office. Because he is placed where it is his duty, and where he has the opportunity, to learn

Reprinted by permission of the publishers from Robert Luce, *Congress: An Explanation,* pp. 46-53. Cambridge, Mass.: Harvard University Press.

more, to study more, and to reflect more, his obligation to inform, to suggest, to advise, and to lead, is all the greater. Therefore law itself may and should help build public opinion.

This does not mean that the lawmaker of to-day is akin to the lawgivers of olden time. He is not to play the part of a Solon or Lycurgus. His opportunities and obligations are not even those of the so-called absolute monarchs of more recent centuries, men who affected to despise or ignore public opinion, though even they could not keep their thrones if they long outraged the views of those immediately about them or the warriors upon whom they depended for support. Fiat law is no longer tolerated. Men have come generally to agree that where the will of the majority is definite and clear, it is to prevail; and where it is indefinite and vague, it must be assumed to be in harmony with the general mass of customs and mental habits. In other words, law must accord with the common sense of the people. Subject to this limitation, the judgment of the legislator may have full scope. If he errs in construing the temper of the people, if he misconceives their needs, his law will not survive. There can be no successful government unless in the end law and public opinion agree.

Furthermore, grave responsibilities are imposed upon the legislator by the fact that the public rarely has any useful opinion in matter of detail. Men may be clear as to purpose without ever giving serious thought to the machinery for accomplishing that purpose. For example, they may object to the use of money in elections, or to the delivery of fireproof coal for furnaces, or to the importation of crop-destroying insects, or to the monopolization of water-power, and yet not have anything like agreement as to how to stop these things. This, you will see, greatly limits the part public opinion plays in legislation, and correspondingly increases that of the legislator. As a matter of fact, it is easily possible to over-emphasize the public opinion phase of legislative work. However, when it does come to the front, it brings to the lawmaker some of his hardest problems and also attracts naturally the most attention from the public, so that it should be further examined.

The most difficult task that confronts the legislator is to find out what may be the preponderance of public opinion on any given topic. I am inclined to think that the harder he works to find this out, the less he accomplishes. At every turn of his activity he invites deception.

He can safely put reliance on no popular vote. Napoleon was

not wide of the mark in declaring: "The first duty of a prince is doubtless to do that which a people wants; but that which a people wants is hardly ever that which it says." Who that has heard a group of ordinarily intelligent men confess how they voted on a number of referenda, and why, can doubt the truth of this? Lack of information is the predominant and sufficient cause. Rare, very rare, is the voter who has acquainted himself with all the facts and who has read or heard thorough argument from both sides. Few, very few, are the men and women who study public questions and who reflect upon what they learn. Most persons have not the leisure, the patience, the training, or the inclination for such tasks. How can it be expected that, when many thousands of the uninformed engage in a plebiscite on other than a few simple questions of broad policy, much weight can be safely attached to the verdict?

Petitions are even more untrustworthy. In the secrecy of the polling booth the voter will exercise his own judgment, if he has any, but when with many others he signs a petition, there is no warrantable presumption that he knows what he is asking or expresses his own view. So many men sign petitions because they are asked and for one reason or another do not want to refuse, that no experienced legislator will dare to put trust in them. That is the reason why they are treated so cavalierly in every legislative body. Congressmen present them out of courtesy and they are listed in the Congressional Record, but their titles are no longer read aloud in the House, and as soon as they reach the committees to which they are referred, they disappear. I have never known a petition to be laid before a committee in session. The brutal fact then is that petitions have no direct effect on legislation. Indirectly they doubtless have some value through acquainting part of the signers with the existence of an agitation for this or that purpose, getting them to think about it, and perhaps enlisting them in that active spread of ideas which finally embodies public opinion in law.

Almost as futile so far as direct effect on Congress is concerned, are the resolutions of state legislatures. Your Congressman is likely to think that he knows as much about the subject involved as the men who voted on the question in the legislature; if it is a national question, it is his duty to know more. Often he has sat in a legislature and well understands how little real thought is there given to resolutions of this character. Those who vote for them risk nothing and may gain favor with somebody. Their votes cannot be safely assumed to reflect the genuine opinion of a majority of their constituents. On the other hand, they invite a real harm, for they give a spineless Congressman the chance to excuse himself by saying he voted this way or that because his state legislature told him so to do.

Resolutions adopted by organizations and associations of all kinds are more substantial, for one may be reasonably confident that as a rule they were not instigated from outside and do convey the real judgment of those who with understanding approved them. When they have been the subject of earnest, informed discussion, they count; but the trouble is that the perfunctory factor is large, and that even where there has been argument, it may have been one-sided, with the decision reached through the influence of zealots.

The printed arguments with which every member of Congress is bombarded—the things we lump under the name of propaganda and with which we surcharge our waste-baskets—rarely show that the authors or signers have studied both sides of the question or have given any thought to contingent considerations. On the other hand, they often do show prejudice, misinformation, or sheer ignorance. Furthermore, they are but fragmentary evidences. The vast and silent majority may feel just the other way.

The newspapers are more helpful. Editorials are the studied work of men more or less informed, who have had some training in the ascertainment and interpretation of the popular mind. It is their business to gather the raw material of public opinion, manufacture it, and sell the product to a public willing to pay for seeing its own ideas in print—sometimes, to be sure, ideas the readers never knew they had, but the ownership of which they will not disavow. Yet editors are no more nearly infallible than Congressmen, and though they help, they do not suffice.

Where, then, shall the lawmaker turn to know what the public really wants? Nowhere, and yet everywhere. If he but talks and listens and reads, a thousand influences will gradually mould his judgment, and presently he will find himself voting as the greater part of his constituents would vote if they had the information and were in his place.

That to my mind is the essence of true representative government. The lawmaker is not to be purely an agent, vainly trying to decide what the majority of his principals desire. He is not to be purely a trustee, making wholly independent decisions, self-conceived and self-sustained. He is to be both agent and trustee as far as may be. He is to feel it as much his duty to try to modify in others opinions with which he disagrees, as to try to let his own opinions be modified by the advice of others. He is to deal fairly both by his constituents and by himself. Such a man deems it necessary to break with constituency or with party only on those very rare occasions when Judgment must step aside and let Conscience rule. The great mass of legislation is matter of expediency. Not once in a thousand times is it matter of what is usually thought of as right and wrong. Only when right and wrong are at stake may the legislator refuse to concede, to compromise, or to yield.

More frequent is the problem when public opinion is in error. Public opinion is not infallible. For this reason it is persuasive, but not compelling. Men in the mass are at times prejudiced, angry, impulsive, unjust. So at times the legislator must stand up against prejudice and passion, impulse and injustice. If resistance to opinion when it is wrong proves unavailing, the legislator should yield his office rather than his judgment. Nothing short of that will bring him peace of mind.

GEORGE B. GALLOWAY

Congressmen Lead and Follow

George B. Galloway has had a distinguished career in research, planning, administration, and teaching. He served as Staff Director of the Joint Congressional Committee on the Organization of Congress in 1945–1946. He has been a member of the Staff Legislative Reference Service of the Library of Congress since 1946. His books include Reform of the Federal Budget (*1950*), The Legislative Process in Congress (*1953*), *Congress and Parliament* (*1955*) *and a* History of the U.S. House of Representatives (*1962*).

. . . [ANOTHER] GREAT FUNCTION of Congress is the two-way task of representing the people in Washington and of informing the people back home about governmental problems. Part of a Congressman's job is to represent the people, in all the diversity of their economic, social, and cultural interests, in the councils of the nation; and to represent the nation and the national interest in the councils of the world while serving as a delegate of the United States at international conferences. Senators represent the states in their equality, and Representatives the multifarious interests of the people in general. It is also part of their job to inform and guide public opinion on the great issues of the day, explaining the pros and cons and debating the merits of proposed courses of action. With the decline of Congress as an original source of legislation, this function of keeping the government in touch with public opinion and of keeping public opinion in touch with the conduct of the public business becomes increasingly important. Congress not only represents the states and districts in the national capital; it also informs the folks back home of national and international problems and how these problems affect them. . . .

From *Congress at the Crossroads*, by George B. Galloway. Copyright 1946 by George B. Galloway. Thomas Y. Crowell Company, New York, publishers.

Despite the hoary antiquity of this representative-informing function, parliamentarians have long differed as to how it should be interpreted and performed. How much independence should an elected representative have? How closely should he keep in touch with the people back home he is supposed to represent? Once a representative is elected, should he follow his own judgment while he is at the seat of government? Or should he always and unquestioningly act and vote just the way the people in his district want him to? Should he deliberately ignore the "popular will" if he thinks it is unintelligent or wrong? Should Congress lead or follow public opinion? How many people take part in the processes of self-government? How big a part do they take? How clear are they about the effect of federal legislation upon themselves and their interests? How familiar are people with reasoned arguments why certain legislation should or should not be passed? In a country as large as the United States and containing so many different types of people, how much unity of public opinion can be expected? . . .

Problem of Parochialism

One question which the conscientious Congressman must often ask himself, especially when conflicts arise between local or regional attitudes and interests and the national welfare, is this: "As a member of Congress, am I merely a delegate from my district or state, restricted to act and vote as the majority which elected me desire, bound by the instructions of my constituents and subservient to their will? Or am I, once elected, a representative of the people of the United States, free to act as I think best for the country generally?"

In a country as large as the United States, with such diverse interests and such a heterogeneous population, the economic interests and social prejudices of particular states and regions often clash with those of other sections and with conceptions of the general interest of the whole nation. The perennial demand of the silver-mining and wool interests in certain western states for purchase and protection, the struggle over slavery, and the recent filibuster of Southern Senators against the attempt to outlaw racial discrimination in employment are familiar examples of recurring conflicts between local interests and prejudices and the common welfare. These political quarrels are rooted in the varying stages of cultural development attained by the different parts of the country. It is the peculiar

task of the politician to compose these differences, to reconcile conflicting national and local attitudes, and to determine when public
opinion is ripe for legislative action. Some conflicts will yield in time
to political adjustment; others must wait for their legal sanction upon
the gradual evolution of the conscience of society. No act of Congress can abolish unemployment or barking dogs or racial prejudices. . . .

TYPES OF PRESSURES ON CONGRESS

One can sympathize with the plight of the conscientious Congressman who is the focal point of all these competing pressures.
The district or state he represents may need and want certain roads,
post offices, courthouses, or schools. Irrigation dams or projects may
be needed for the development of the area's resources. If the representative is to prove himself successful in the eyes of the people
back home, he must be able to show, at least occasionally, some
visible and concrete results of his congressional activity. Or else he
must be able to give good reasons why he has not been able to
carry out his pledges. The local residence rule for Congressmen
multiplies the pressures that impinge upon him. Faithful party
workers who have helped elect him will expect the Congressman to
pay his political debts by getting them jobs in the federal service.
Constituents affected by proposed legislation may send him an
avalanche of letters, telegrams, and petitions which must be acknowledged and followed up. The region from which he comes will
expect him to protect and advance its interests in Washington. All
the various organized groups will press their claims upon him and
threaten him if he does not jump when they crack the whip. Party
leaders may urge a Congressman to support or oppose the Administration program or to "trade" votes for the sake of party harmony
or various sectional interests. He is also under pressure from his
own conscience as to what he should do both to help the people
who have elected him and to advance the best interests of the
nation. Besieged by all these competing pressures, a Congressman is
often faced with the choice of compromising between various pressures, of trading votes, of resisting special interests of one sort or
another, of staying off the floor when a vote is taken on some
measure he prefers not to take a stand on, of getting support here
and at the same time running the risk of losing support there.
Dealing with pressure blocs is a problem in political psychology
which involves a careful calculation of the power of the blocs,

the reaction of the voters on election day, and the long-haul interests of the district, state, and nation. . . .

SHOULD CONGRESS LEAD OR FOLLOW PUBLIC OPINION?

It is axiomatic to say that in a democracy public opinion is the source of law. Unless legislation is sanctioned by the sense of right of the people, it becomes a dead letter on the statute books, like prohibition and the Hatch Act. But public opinion is a mercurial force; now quiescent, now vociferous, it has various moods and qualities. It reacts to events and is often vague and hard to weigh.

Nor is public opinion infallible. Most people are naturally preoccupied with their personal problems and daily affairs; national problems and legislative decisions seem complex and remote to them, despite press and radio and occasional Capitol tours. Comparatively few adults understand the technicalities of foreign loans or reciprocal trade treaties, although congressional action on these aspects of our foreign economic policy may have far-reaching effects upon our standard of living. . . .

In practice, a Congressman both leads and follows public opinion. The desires of his constituents, of his party, and of this or that pressure group all enter into his decisions on matters of major importance. The influence of these factors varies from member to member and measure to measure. Some Congressmen consider it their duty to follow closely what they think is the majority opinion of their constituents, especially just before an election. Others feel that they should make their decisions without regard to their constituents' wishes in the first place, and then try to educate and convert them afterwards. Some members are strong party men and follow more or less blindly the program of the party leaders. Except when they are very powerful in the home district, the pressure groups are more of a nuisance than a deciding influence on the average member. When a legislator is caught between the conflicting pressures of his constituents and his colleagues, he perforce compromises between them and follows his own judgment.

The average legislator discovers early in his career that certain interests or prejudices of his constituents are dangerous to trifle with. Some of these prejudices may not be of fundamental importance to the welfare of the nation, in which case he is justified in humoring them, even though he may disapprove. The difficult case occurs where the prejudice concerns some fundamental policy affecting the national welfare. A sound sense of values, the ability to discriminate between that which is of fundamental importance and that which is only superficial, is an indispensable qualification of a good legislator.

Senator Fulbright gives an interesting example of this distinction in his stand on the poll-tax issue and isolationism. "Regardless of how persuasive my colleagues or the national press may be about the evils of the poll tax, I do not see its fundamental importance, and I shall follow the views of the people of my state. Although it may be symbolic of conditions which many deplore, it is exceedingly doubtful that its abolition will cure any of our major problems. On the other hand, regardless of how strongly opposed my constituents may prove to be to the creation of, and participation in, an ever stronger United Nations Organization, I could not follow such a policy in that field unless it becomes clearly hopeless."[1]

A TWO-WAY JOB

As believers in democracy, probably most Americans would agree that it is the duty of Congressmen to follow public opinion insofar as it expresses the desires, wants, needs, aspirations, and ideals of the people. Most Americans probably would also consider it essential for their representatives to make as careful an appraisal of these needs and desires as they can, and to consider, in connection with such an appraisal, the ways and means of accomplishing them. Legislators have at hand more information about legal structures, economic problems, productive capacities, manpower possibilities, and the like, than the average citizen they represent. They can draw upon that information to inform and lead the people— by showing the extent to which their desires can be realized.

In other words, a true representative of the people would follow the people's desires and at the same time lead the people in formulating ways of accomplishing those desires. He would lead the people in the sense of calling to their attention the difficulties of achieving those aims and the ways to overcome the difficulties. This means also that, where necessary, he would show special interest groups or even majorities how, according to his own interpretation and his own conscience, their desires need to be tempered in the common interest or for the future good of the nation.

Thus the job of a Congressman is a two-way one. He represents his local area and interests in the national capital, and he also in-

[1] In an address on "The Legislator" delivered at the University of Chicago on February 19, 1946. *Vital Speeches,* May 15, 1946, pp. 468–472.

forms the people back home of problems arising at the seat of government and how these problems affect them. It is in the nature of the Congressman's job that he should determine, as far as he can, public opinion in his own constituency and in the whole nation, analyze it, measure it in terms of the practicability of turning it into public policy, and consider it in the light of his own knowledge, conscience, and convictions. Occasionally he may be obliged to go against public opinion, with the consequent task of educating or re-educating the people along lines that seem to him more sound. And finally, since he is a human being eager to succeed at his important job of statesmanship and politics, he is realistic enough to keep his eyes on the voters in terms of the next election. But he understands that a mere weather-vane following of majority public opinion is not always the path to reelection.

WILDER W. CRANE, JR.

All Legislators Are Politicos

Wilder Crane is Professor of Political Science at The University of Wisconsin, Milwaukee. He served as an Assemblyman in the Wisconsin Legislature, 1957–58. He is the author of American State Legislatures (*1967*), The Legislature of Lower Austria (*1961*), *co-author with Alex N. Dragnich and John C. Wahlke and others of* Government and Politics (*1966*), *and contributing author of* The Politics of Reapportionment (*1962*). *This article, "Styles of Representation and Legislative Decisions," is drawn from Professor Crane's prize-winning doctoral dissertation, "The Legislative Struggle in Wisconsin: Decision Making in the 1957 Wisconsin Assembly," Madison, The University of Wisconsin, 1959.*

SINCE EDMUND BURKE expounded his position on his dilemma as representative from Bristol, there has been much discussion of the normative question of how a legislator ought to vote. Little research has been undertaken, however, to indicate how role concepts relate to decisions actually made by legislators. Thus, this article may contribute something to understanding whether normative concepts of representation are reflected in decisions made by legislators. This writer is convinced that, regardless of how legislators may answer questions concerning normative concepts of style of representation, all of them are politicos. Whether they say they are trustees voting on the merits of bills, delegates voting in accordance with demands of districts or interest groups, or partisans voting in accordance with perceived positions of their political party, they are actually all politicos, who vote on differing bases depending on the issues confronting them.

The basis for this article is a study of the 1957 Assembly, the

From Wilder W. Crane, Jr., "The Legislative Struggle in Wisconsin: Decision Making in the 1957 Wisconsin Assembly" (Madison, 1959). Reprinted by permission of the author.

lower house of the Wisconsin Legislature. Eighty-one members, a statistically valid sample of the total one hundred members, were asked why they had voted as they did on twenty issues. The twenty decisions were chosen as examples, but not statistically accurate samples, of the different kinds of issues confronting legislators on roll calls. They included bills categorized by the author and a panel of experts as major public policy, party conflict, interest group conflict, rural-urban conflict, local and geographic conflict restricted to one area of the state, and bills so minor that very few people outside the legislature were aware of them. The legislator respondents were asked to explain the reasons for their votes on these issues.

Their replies indicate that no legislator explained his votes on all twenty issues on the same basis. Not one respondent, for example, stated that he had voted on his concept of the merits of all proposals. While some studies classify some legislators as trustees, it hardly seems possible that these 1957 Wisconsin Assemblymen could have voted on the merits of all 1072 roll calls conducted. Nor could they have voted as delegates on issues on which no perceived geographic interest or interest group provided any instructions. Nor could they have voted as partisans, when the parties were often divided on critical issues and thus failed to provide cue-giving mechanisms. Rather, each legislator voted on different bases depending on the nature of the issues. While some were more inclined to give vote explanations based on a trustee orientation, others were more inclined to give explanations based on delegate or partisan orientations, but no respondent consistently explained all of his decisions on any one basis.

The bills selected for the study had a higher visibility than a statistical sample of bills would have had; thus, more votes were cast on the merits of the issues than would have been the case with a statistical sample of bills. Nonetheless, less than half the vote explanations, specifically 45%, were based on explanations reflecting a trustee's concepts of the merits of the proposals. This was the case, although the coding system gave all the benefit to trustee votes. All other vote explanations were coded in accordance with a standard that required that the respondent indicate that he had voted in the absence of his convictions or contrary to his convictions.

The total vote explanations given by eighty-one respondents on twenty bills are presented in Table I.

TABLE I
VOTE EXPLANATIONS OF LEGISLATORS
CATEGORIZED ACCORDING TO
REPRESENTATIONAL CONCEPTS OF STYLE
1957 Wisconsin Assembly

Trustee	45%
Delegate (District or Interest Group)	22%
Partisan	$14\frac{1}{2}$%
Legislator	11%
Others (logrolling, prejudice, adverse reaction to pressure, etc.)	$7\frac{1}{2}$%

The explanations of respondents of their votes indicate the differing bases on which they voted on different issues. Examples of these different types of explanations follow:

TRUSTEE VOTE
I felt, if the northern counties would be helped, OK. I used my own judgment. I felt that was the equitable way, I felt it was the American moral way of looking at things.

DELEGATE VOTE
(*District Delegate*) If my district loses that much money, I can't go along with the party.

(*Interest Group Delegate*) I had pressure and nobody pressured me on the other side. I took the line of least resistance.

PARTISAN VOTE
In my own heart, I wasn't really for it. I thought that following the Governor might help the party.

Trustee, delegate, and partisan votes are to be expected among those reading the normative literature in political science. However, what this empirical study determined is that some votes are cast on a purely personal basis which reflects neither the legislator's concepts of the merits of a proposal nor any concept of his that he is representing anyone else. Such votes reflect the extent to which the legislature is an *institution* with its own group relationships and is not simply a device for representing others. Such votes are categorized in this study as *Legislator Votes,* examples of which include the following vote explanations:

Vic Wallin's pet. I voted on account of him, not on account of the bill's merits.

No special reason. Because of Danielson himself; he was a little sassy.

Every type of bill encountered every type of representational response described here, but different types of bills encountered different patterns of response. Respondents were asked whether they were "concerned" about bills, and the correlation between their stating that they were concerned and their giving trustee vote explanations is statistically significant. Trustee vote explanations were given by over half the respondents on the one major public policy bill, one local bill, and five interest group conflict bills.

Partisan vote explanations, on the other hand, were correlated with a low degree of concern about issues. The majority of respondents gave partisan vote explanations on the one issue categorized as partisan. However, what is most striking about partisan vote explanations is that there were many partisan responses to all other categories of bills. While it is obvious that local and minor bills may encounter partisan responses among legislators not concerned about the merits, it is more interesting to note that some interest group conflicts and some rural-urban conflicts resulted in partisan vote explanations.

Delegate vote explanations were given most often on rural-urban conflicts and interest group conflicts. In most cases, votes cast were consistent with what the legislators perceived as the strongest external pressure, although in a few cases, legislators became provoked by what they regarded as undue pressure and voted against interest group bills to which they had no objection on the merits. It is also worth noting that vote explanations on a district delegate basis were correlated with urban-rural conflict, whereas partisan votes were cast on issues not regarded by the legislators as partisan. It appears that rural-urban conflict is an "unnatural" factionalism based on conscious decisions, whereas partisan voting is sustained by other cue-giving mechanisms not perceived by the legislators as partisan.

The politico role was recognized by the authors of the four state study:

"Both role orientations—that of trustee and that of delegate—may be held serially, depending on whether the legislator's focus is centered on one clientele or another. For instance, he may see himself as a delegate in matters of local interest, and as a trustee in all other matters. . . . Or the legislator may feel that he must follow his party's instructions in political matters, though on others he can be a free agent."[1]

What this study of Wisconsin indicates is that all legislators are politicos, who shift representational concepts depending on the issues. And sometimes, they simply vote their reactions to fellow legislators without any concept of representing anyone, not even themselves.

[1] John C. Wahlke, Heinz Eulau, William Buchanan, and Leroy C. Ferguson, *The Legislative System* (New York: Wiley, 1962), p. 278.

FRANK J. SORAUF

Lawmakers Make No Firm Commitment

Frank Sorauf is Professor of Political Science at The University of Minnesota. Party and Representation, *from which the following selection is taken, won an American Political Science Association Prize in 1962. Among Professor Sorauf's other books are* Political Parties in the American System (*1964*) *and* Political Science: An Informal Overview (*1965*).

In 1938, *Fortune* MAGAZINE approached a sample of the American electorate with the question: "Do you believe that a congressman should vote on any question as the majority of his constituents desire, or vote according to his own judgment?" More than 54 per cent of the respondents chose "his own judgment," and more than 37 per cent declared for the constituency. The remainder offered no opinion.[1] Some twenty years later, a team of political scientists questioning the legislators themselves in four states found that 63 per cent identified themselves with a "trustee" role very similar to *Fortune's* "own-judgment" alternative.[2]

The results of these two studies illustrate the problem of defining the legislative role. They indicate that a majority of both governors and governed formally subscribe to the image of the

[1] "The Fortune Survey," *Fortune,* XVIII (1938), No. 5, 96; quoted in Alfred de Grazia, *Public and Republic* (New York: A. A. Knopf, 1951), p. 158.

[2] Heinz Eulau, John Wahlke, William Buchanan, and Leroy Ferguson, "The Role of the Representative: Some Empirical Observations on the Theory of Edmund Burke," *American Political Science Review,* LIII (1959), No. 3, 742–756. The authors break the legislative role into two dimensions, one of "style" focus (trustee, delegate, and politico), the other of "area" focus (district, state, district-plus-state). However, the delegate in style coincides, as one might expect, with the district-area focus. He directs his responsibilities to the district which chose him rather than to the state as a whole.

From Frank J. Sorauf, *Party and Representation: Legislative Politics in Pennsylvania* (New York, 1963), pp. 122–128, 132–133. Reprinted by permission of the Publishers, Atherton Press. Copyright © 1963, Atherton Press, New York. All rights reserved.

legislator as a free, unfettered decision-maker, drawing his wisdom chiefly, if not completely, from his own virtue, knowledge, and experience. The vernacular of our politics has, in fact, a series of unflattering epithets for the legislator who has surrendered that independent spirit to either party or constituency. He is a "cat's-paw," a "rubber stamp," a "lackey." Given this attitude, no dispute, one assumes, could rage here between a Burke and his Bristol. Yet do these formal protestations reflect the real expectations of constituents and of legislators? Most legislators know too well how quickly their constituents turn against them when they differ from their representative's "independent" judgment. Formal attributions of role aside, they must conjure with the demands and scrutiny of their electors.

To determine their solution to the cross-pressures of constituency, party, and personal commitment, the Pennsylvania legislative candidates of this study were asked several open-ended questions about their legislative role.[3] On the basis of their extended responses, they were categorized three times: once on their resolution of the district-wishes—versus—own-judgment conflict, once by the degree of party loyalty expressed, and once by their general ranking of constituency, party, and own judgment in their over-all concept of the legislative role. Table 1 reports the general results.

Contrary to the four-state study mentioned above, only 31.1 per cent of the Pennsylvania legislative candidates declared clearly for their personal judgment (the trustee role) in the event of its conflict with their constituents' wishes. Even when one takes only those candidates who chose a clear alternative, the percentage of trustees rises to only 45.8. The discrepancy between these two studies may be explained on several grounds. The localism that ties a legislator to his constituents flourishes in Pennsylvania, more widely perhaps than in comparable states. "Servicing the constituents" absorbs an important part of every legislator's attention. The representative with pockets full of driver's-license applications for his personal processing is not an uncommon sight in the General Assembly. Many legislative campaigns are fought on the issue of what the incumbent legislator did or did not "get" for the district in the two years of his stewardship. Every errand run in Harrisburg, every

[3] The three opening questions were: "Do you think a legislator should be primarily guided by the wishes of his district, of his party, or by his own judgment?" "What should he do if his district wants one thing, and he believes in another?" "How much loyalty do you think a legislator owes his party?" They were often followed by additional clarifying and probing questions.

TABLE 1

EXPRESSIONS OF LEGISLATIVE ROLE BY 1958
LEGISLATIVE CANDIDATES

	Legislators		Defeated candidates	
	Dem. (N = 54)	Rep. (N = 52)	Dem. (N = 52)	Rep. (N = 54)
	PERCENTAGE			
I. CONSTITUENCY VERSUS JUDGMENT				
Constituency ("delegate")	35.2	42.3	30.8	38.9
Own judgment ("trustee")	40.7	25.0	34.6	24.1
Compromise, evasion	24.1	30.8	32.7	18.5
No information	0	1.9	1.9	18.5
II. DEGREE OF PARTY LOYALTY				
Hostile, weak	5.6	7.7	15.4	25.9
Moderate	48.1	57.7	59.6	46.3
Strong	42.6	28.8	19.2	9.3
No information	3.7	5.8	5.8	18.5
III. GENERAL ROLE				
Party-oriented	11.1	5.8	3.8	1.9
District-oriented	35.2	55.8	34.6	38.9
Self-oriented	31.5	19.2	40.4	29.6
None discernible	22.0	17.3	19.2	11.1
No information	0	1.9	1.9	18.5

patronage job garnered for a constituent, every road paved or re-paved in the district scores valuable points in the home town or county. The strength of these local demands may reflect the height-ened needs of the failing and depressed sectors of the state. Like the feverish demands for patronage, they may reflect the politics of declining prosperity in which the benefits of the state assume a growing importance. And, like the demands for patronage, they reflect a political style built on immediate, direct rewards to the participants.

The lower incidence of "trustees" in Pennsylvania may also re-flect the complex and equivocating answers these questions elicited. A number asserted that conflicts between their districts and their judgments were rare. "A man usually agrees with his district, since he's one of them and typical of them," one legislator noted. An-other reported that his main problem was in getting any response— even one of opposition—from his urban district: "It's hard to get

them to think about anything happening down here in Harrisburg."
Others whisked the problem away with a little semantic trickery. "A
representative's judgment," according to one, "should arise from
knowing the needs and wants of his district and state." The choice
between district and personal judgment is an artificial issue for
many legislators. They have no really clear or elaborate ideological
guides or thought-out positions which encumber them as they
decide between a "yea" and a "nay." Furthermore, they are so much
creatures of their constituencies that they share its goals and values
fully. The value of this classic dilemma in representative theory
may, in other words, be chiefly heuristic.

Just where party fits into legislative choice in Pennsylvania appears to be, by the candidates' wishes, a separable problem. When
confronted with the question of party as against constituency and
own judgment as sources of legislative responsibility, only two (one
incumbent of each party) of the 200 responding legislators chose
party. Doubtless the social, and even political, unacceptability of
such a response was crucial. Certainly, this virtually unanimous un-
willingness to admit the guidance of party stands at odds with the
considerable amount of party discipline in the Pennsylvania legislature. And, since that discipline . . . is greater among the Democrats, one may wonder whether their preference for personal
judgment over district guidance might not mask commitments to
party.

In identifying their own degree of party loyalty, many candidates
and legislators saw no great conflict between party and their commitment to constituency and self. The party to which they pledge
fealty is usually the local constituency party, a semiautonomous
political barony sensitive to the desires of its constituents. Its main
concerns are local improvements and patronage, and it is only
rarely stirred to support a state-wide party program or gubernatorial
administration. Also widespread among the interviewees was a purely
pragmatic approach to party loyalty—one supports the party to
the degree necessary to win the party's electoral support and to the
degree to which that support is crucial for victory. Any number of
rural-legislators explained their tenuous ties to party simply in terms
of the party's doing little for them at election-time.

We have thus far assumed that the legislators' choices reflect the
threefold pressures of party, constituency, and self. To put it that
baldly, of course, overlooks the complexity of these three sources of
legislative responsibility. Constituency party may conflict with

legislative party, and the legislator's loyalties to his occupational interest may contradict his awareness of those broader interests which he calls "the public interest" in his statesmanlike moments.

The average legislator appears, then, to make no firm commitment to constituency, party, or self. Their demands on him and their sanctions over him shift from issue to issue. Both the shifting political demands and the finely balanced equities of choice force him to choose only tentatively and cautiously, one issue at a time. Yet, there is a handful of legislators and defeated candidates who approach that artificial construct, the pure type, and who vest their legislative responsibility almost exclusively in one of the three sources. Small though their number is, they afford useful illustrations in human terms of the three extreme dimensions of the legislative role. A composite and fictional picture of each, based largely on two or three cases, follows.

Rep. George Williams, the "delegate" par excellence, is as closely wedded to his legislative constituency as any man in Harrisburg. Catering to its every fleeting wish has been the story of his legislative career. His constituency—a homogeneous, somewhat provincial farming county in the central section of the state—adheres to a traditional two-party politics having little about them of the ideological currents of the past thirty years. It draws party lines largely along old family and clan lines, and it expects only that a state legislator tend to local demands. Williams, a merchant whose business keeps him in contact with the rural folks of the county, does exactly that. "I know I've done more for my people than any other representative this county has ever had," he proclaims proudly. "I've found out what they wanted and tried to get it for them." Fairly wealthy by local standards, he has few organizational memberships in the county seat and has little truck with social circles there. His ties are closer to the out-county people, to whom he is a fixer, friend, patron, and confidant. He is especially adept in finding patronage jobs in Harrisburg for the people of the county (regardless of party), and he willingly intercedes with distant authority (such as the Bureau of Motor Vehicles) when it threatens a local resident. On a somewhat broader scale, Williams works tirelessly to bring light industry into the county to offset the decline in farm production. His political success may be marked by the fact that he has won four terms in the House, breaking the tradition of "two terms and out" for the county's legislator. His political success has naturally made him a power in his party's county committee, but party remains for him at best a concerted expression of the wishes of the constituency.

The errand-boy role, however, holds little appeal for Rep. John Gibbons. Although his constituency is not so completely rural as Williams', it is not vastly different. Gibbons, however, is an *idéologue* and the epitome of the "trustee" in legislative affairs. In an interview, his voice tends to rise, and his speech inclines to finger-poking, conversational oratory. "We've gotten too far away from principle—government and politics are too expedient—too much giving away and too many promises to get votes. We need a new set of guiding principles." His principles, however, are general, moralistic, and nonpolitical: running government "like a big business," reforming the laws and the constitution of the state, getting "the incompetents" (apparently the patronage holders) out of state government. In his county, he maintains a law practice and active community ties—the Rotary, Little League, and the Masons. And yet he resists constituency pressures with the conviction that the majority is not always right and that the legislator must above all not yield his "conscience" to any man. Only the fact that he, as a lifelong resident of the county, is so steeped in its needs and values saves him from disastrous independence. As it is, grumbling mounts within the county about his inattention to mail and phone calls, and many voters can tick off the last, distant year in which a new road was built in the county. To his party he accords only an uncertain loyalty. "I won't wear the party chains like many in the House," he claims.

Belonging to an even rarer species, the unalloyed "partisan," Frank Naughton represents two thickly settled metropolitan wards. In a lower-middle-class ward in which first- and second-generation Irish Catholics predominate, he is a lifelong resident and an Irish Catholic. He has worked as a precinct committeeman for seventeen years, and since his election to the House some seven years ago he has been a ward leader. His father had earlier been active in local politics for more than twenty-five years, and Naughton today thrives, as his father did, amid the intricate, Byzantine convolutions of the urban political machine. His friends come exclusively from the party and from the labor-union circles to which his sometime occupation as a tool-and-die–maker gives him access. The world of social and fraternal organizations attracts him very little. His role as faithful party follower is, then, not unexpected. The party organization tapped him as a candidate for the legislature, although he had never before run for public office, and the party vote elected him and continues to elect him to the House. "They [the party]," he explains, "have the greatest insight into the wishes of the district. I owe them 100 per-cent loyalty—I wouldn't be here if it wasn't for the party." This is not to say, though, that Naughton is inattentive to his constituents or even to the general interests of labor and the common man. He serves them through service to the party.

Atypical though Williams, Gibbons, and Naughton are, they represent the three "legislators" who battle for recognition within every member of the House. Peculiarities of constituency and their personal ideologies have made it possible for them to choose one of the three with unusual certainty and consistency. But to a greater degree, their single course or role is but a verbalism, a recognition that, for them, at least two of the three options frequently coincide. The man of little education and even less experience in formulating ideologies and in whose constituency party organization is little more than a local booster club can, for instance, opt for the single role of "delegate" with few qualms and considerable impunity. . . .

Inconclusive though they may be, these self-evaluations of legislative role do scotch one old and one recent suggestion about legislative role. No evidence here supports the recent proposition that representatives now increasingly define their job in the "trustee" dimension because constituent control over their activities is increasingly thwarted by the intricacy and obscurity of contemporary governmental issues.[4] Party and constituency influences remain potent in Pennsylvania, and in adopting a posture as an elected representative the members of the House acknowledge that fact. Even as issues of public policy become forbiddingly complex for the citizen, so do they also for the only slightly more experienced state legislator. He may be increasingly happy to accept the cues and leadership of an all-knowing party or of knowledgeable constituents. Since the average state legislator legislates only as a part-time, semiprofessional representative, competing policy alternatives may confuse and confound him as readily as they do his constituents.

[4] Eulau et al., *op. cit.,* among others, make this point.

II

The Representative in Perspective

CHARLES A. BEARD AND
JOHN D. LEWIS

Representative Government in Evolution

Charles A. Beard, 1874–1948, was a towering figure in both history and political science. Always provocative, always readable, he served as President of both the American Political Science Association (1926) and the American Historical Association (1933), and left his mark on Twentieth Century America with a host of books and articles of which An Economic Interpretation of the Constitution *(1913),* The Economic Origins of Jeffersonian Democracy *(1915), and (with Mary R. Beard)* The Rise of American Civilization *(4 Vols., 1927–1942) are the most influential.*

John D. Lewis is Professor of Political Science at Oberlin College. He is the author of The Genossenschaft Theory of Otto von Gierke *(1935), co-author of* Democracy is Different *(1941),* The Study of Comparative Government *(1949), and* Against the Tyrant *(1957).*

REPRESENTATIVE GOVERNMENT on a national scale did not originate in the psychology of primitive Teutons, as English historians long contended; nor is it a mere bourgeois institution of passing significance, designed to delude the masses, as Fascists and Bolsheviks have alleged. Its vast historical complications conform to no such simple thesis. On the contrary, representative government began

From Charles A. Beard and John D. Lewis, "Representative Government in Evolution," *The American Political Science Review,* Vol. XXVI, No. 2 (April, 1932), pp. 223–240. Reprinted by permission of the American Political Science Association and of John D. Lewis.

its career as an instrument of political power, in a given complex of social and economic circumstances, to serve the purposes of ruling monarchs; and it has played a bewildering rôle, in form, spirit, and authority, for more than five hundred years. Flexibility has been its prime characteristic. As a means, not an end in itself, it has served an infinite variety of causes, and has displayed both adaptability and survival power. In form, it has not been a political stereotype. Rather, it has been amazingly variable. In spirit, in the ideas associated with its evolution, and in the uses to which it may be put, representative government is subtle and adaptable, offering to statesmen who have imagination and manipulative capacity a tool of inexhaustible utility. Hence a wide historical view of representative government in evolution is indispensable to any understanding of its nature or its possible place in the future government of mankind.

It is fitting to inquire at the outset rather narrowly into the concept, or idea, of representation—a term that is used freely in political literature as if the thing for which it stands were an objective reality, the same always and everywhere. Unfortunately, this is a difficult task. The writer in the field of politics labors under difficulties which do not vex his colleagues in natural science. The latter are concerned primarily with objective phenomena that do not change rapidly with the seasons and are not associated with fuzzy ideas, at least not immediately; hydrogen was hydrogen to Lord Kelvin and is still hydrogen to Madam Curie. The student of politics, on the other hand, must deal with phenomena which are both ideas and realities. He has before him, let us say, a parliament of 450 members, all of whom may be described fairly well in anthropometric terms and speak for given numbers of persons statistically measurable in the election returns. But such facts are relatively unimportant. The action of this parliament springs from ideas, wills, sentiments, and ambitions within individual members, acting in response to complex stimuli from without. Description and measurement, at all events in the present state of our discernment, do not give us an understanding of representation.

If the idea of representation could be caught on the wing, transfixed, and dissected at a given moment, the troubles of the searcher would not be at an end. Every political idea is in process of continuous evolution. It changes from time to time as its possessors give new content to it out of inquiry and experience. And at a particular moment it may mean one thing to the logically competent and something else to the more or less obfuscated generality. To this rule, the conception of representation offers no exception. It evolves in structure and spirit, precisely as the institution itself is confronted by new tasks thrown up by the social and economic development of the society in which it functions.

For these reasons, and many others, it is appropriate to ask first of all: What realities are covered by the word "representation"? The term has come into the English language through French derivatives from the Latin *repraesentare,* meaning, quite literally, "to bring before one, to bring back, to exhibit, to show, to manifest, to display." In classical Latin, it was not a political term, but was applied primarily to concrete objects, in a very realistic fashion. When it appeared in England, after a sojourn in France, transformed through *représentation,* its original meaning still clung to it. In fourteenth-century English, it meant "to symbolise, to serve as a visible and concrete embodiment of;" as, for example, in Wycliffe: "Ymages that representen pompe and glorie of the worlde."

No illustrations of its use in a political sense appear before the sixteenth century, at least in the record of the Oxford Dictionary. By that time, it had come to mean to take or fill the place of another in some capacity or for some purpose; to be a substitute in some capacity for another person or body; to act for another by deputed right. "Our Generall," runs a quotation from about 1595, "sent Cap. Jobson, repraesenting his person with his authority, as his Leiftenante Generall." Speaking strictly, of course, this is not a political usage, but it implies agency, deputation, and authorization, and hence marks an easy transition to the purely political terminology employed by such writers as Coke, Hobbes, and Locke. Doubtless the English transformation was facilitated by the fact that during the early Middle Ages *repraesentare* had acquired, in the hands of Latin writers, a political meaning akin to its present sense. However this may be, representation had come into general use in England by the opening of the seventeenth century to describe the system of deputation that had grown up with the development of Parliament.

But in time the term took on more mystic implications. Near the close of the sixteenth century, Sir Thomas Smith could write that the Parliament of England "representeth and hath the power of the whole realme both the head and the bodie. For everie Englishman is entended to be there present, either by person or by procuration and attornies, of whatever preheminence, state, dignitie, or qualities soever he be, from the Prince (be he King or Queen) to the lowest person of England, and the consent of Parliament is taken to be everie man's consent." This concept Burke carried another step: "The value, spirit, and essence of the House of Commons consists in its being the express image of the feelings of the nation." In other words, the idea of representation has in it the concept of bare agency, the substitution of one for many, but it is more: the supreme representative body is supposed to mirror the whole movement of social and economic forces within the nation, to express the nation's will and its sentiments. Correctly conceived, it involves a philosophy of history.

Although representative government now carries with it such democratic implications, it has not always been democratic in conception. Some of the mediaeval writers looked upon the absolute monarch as *representing* the community. According to John of Salisbury, "the prince is first of all to make a thorough survey of himself, and diligently study the condition of the whole body of the commonwealth of which he is the representative, and in whose place he stands. . . ." Again: "Wherefore in the ordinances of princes or the promulgations of magistrates the plural number is used by prolemsis to the end that every ordinance and other kind of promulgation may be seen to be the act not so much of the officer personally as of the corporate community. . . ." In John's political theory, the prince is the representative of the community—in other words, stands in the place of the community. Owing to his representative character, the acts of the prince are to be deemed acts of the community. Yet while he acts for the generality, he is not responsible to the commonwealth for what he does. As Dickinson puts it, "the prince is responsible *for* the commonwealth, but not *to* it." Since he holds his office from God rather than the people, he is responsible only to God or to God's representatives. Later mediaeval writers make use of a similar concept of representation; and the controversies over conflicting authority are often expressed in terms of rival representative capacities.

If we leave speculative writers for concrete realities, we also find representation often disassociated from democratic notions. A representative body may speak for a narrow class, as did the English parliament for about six hundred years. Neither does it carry with it republican implications; England has retained her monarchy through all the vicissitudes of parliamentary development, save for a brief period in the seventeenth century. There are additional limitations on the doctrine in practice. The Fathers of the American Constitution believed in representative and republican government, but they feared the populace as they feared original sin. One of their fundamental purposes in shaping the form of the federal government was to break the force of majority rule at its source in elections and in the operation of the government itself. In itself, therefore, representative government need not be republican or democratic. It may be monarchical, or aristocratic, or so designed as to prevent the kind of popular government which operates through simple majorities.

Yet, despite these difficulties of definition, we may say, for the sake of convenience, that the modern idea of representation can be broken into three component parts: (1) a representative person or group has power to act for, or in place of, another person or group; (2) the representative is elected by those for whom he is to act; (3) the representative is responsible for his acts to those whom he represents.

But this analysis is not at bottom as simple as it seems on the surface, and should not be allowed to stand without a caveat. What is this power which resides in the constituency or body politic and is transferred in whole or in part to the representative? At best, it is an elusive fluid. What methods of nomination and election are established by law to govern choice by the voters, and how do they operate in practice? What is responsibility in essence, and how is it to be enforced? Obviously, the representative is more than an agent in the private law sense of the term. He helps to make the ideas and wills which he represents. Often he has to deal with issues which his constituents have scarcely considered, if at all —issues on which they have expressed no will. Hence, when we define representative government in simple terms, as above, we arbitrarily lay out a little land of rational certainty and speak in the language of anatomy. This is not enough, for representative government is merely one phase of the whole process of civilization, and those who speak of it as if it were a Victorian bustle, to be put on or entirely discarded at will, display a woeful ignorance of its history and nature.

From what has been said about the history of the word representation, it may readily be imagined that the philosophy of representative government was unknown to the ancients and but dimly foreshadowed by the writers of the Middle Ages. During the thousands of years which we call antiquity, monarchies, despotisms, dictatorships, tyrannies, democracies, and aristocracies, with numerous variants, rose, flourished, and fell; but nowhere, at no time, did representative institutions appear, at least on any impressive scale. Aristotle, the father of political science, does, indeed, refer once to the fact that democracies, such as existed at Mantinea, did exercise the power of electing magistrates, and thus acted "through representatives elected in turn out of the whole people;" but this reference is casual, and is made in a tone which suggests that the case is exceptional. A modern writer on political philosophy, Jellinek, while claiming that Greek magistrates were regarded as representatives in the execution of policies adopted by popular assemblies, admits that the Greeks had no notion of representation as applied to the creation of legislative assemblies. Even if his first point be conceded, namely, that Greek magistrates were representative in character, it is significant to note that Aristotle lays no great stress on the conception.

In Roman, as well as in Greek, thinking, the idea of representation in government appears only in shadowy forms. Polybius, it is true, speaks of the responsibility of the consuls to the senate and to the people, of the responsibility of the senate to the people, and of the responsibility of the tribunes to the people. Certain passages in Roman law have also been interpreted to imply that the senate was representative in character, that is, spoke for others who were not members of that body. But Polybius does not look upon the Roman officers of state as agents or representatives of the people; nor does the actual composition of the Roman senate lend any color to the view that it was representative in any modern sense, or indeed any strict sense, of the word.

This does not mean, of course, that the theory and practice of agency was unknown to the ancients. "The city," says Ernest Barker, "was not devoid of representative institutions, nor unacquainted with the political machinery which is connected with those institutions." He cites the Athenian council as an example of an elected representative assembly, but admits that it did not have "representative authority," that is, authority "to deliberate and decide as the exponent of the general will within its sphere." Again, the synod of the Bœotian League "consisted of 660 members, elected in equal numbers from the eleven electoral divisions of the League;" but that was more of a diplomatic assembly than a legislature in the modern sense. While it would not be correct to say, therefore, that representation was utterly foreign to Greek and

Roman politics, practical illustrations of it were few and must be strained to make any case worthy of serious attention. At all events, modern legislative bodies have no historic connections with Greek and Roman representative agencies.

The starting point of representative government on a national scale, then, is the Middle Ages in time, and the place is Europe. It did not spring up because people suddenly decided to govern themselves, displayed the capacity, and set up parliaments. It was called into being by mediaeval monarchs who had established or maintained by the sword political power over wide territorial areas containing a large population socially aggregated into classes and groups and communities. The monarchs who first called representatives of communities or estates to grant money and give counsel were not thinking of democracy; they were concerned primarily with the conservation of the peace, the administration of lucrative justice, and the replenishment of their royal treasuries. Even the most despotic mediaeval monarch could not tax and exploit his subjects without limits; as a matter of expediency also, he had to consider ways and means. The estates and classes that composed the social order under him had interests and sentiments which he could not ignore, save at great peril to himself; and a certain degree of coöperation with them offered the most effective method of gaining his immediate ends. Beyond that he could not see, for practical men are adjusters, not prophets.

The rest of the record is equally clear. Although the several phases are familiar to students of constitutional history, it seems fitting to set down here, in summary form, for purposes of illustration, the principal stages in the development of representative government in England.

1. The first parliaments were called by monarchs primarily for the purpose of voting taxes for the royal treasury. The original parliament did not represent people—free and equal heads—as such, but the estates of the realm (the nobility, clergy, landed gentry, and burgesses of the towns); in a strict economic sense, two estates, i.e., land and commerce. In the early assemblies, there was some talking about ways and means of raising revenues (hence the term "parliament"); but discussion was an incident, not a prime end.

2. In time, the tax-voting body became a law-making body, by gradual steps. The members of the estates who were being consulted and taxed had grievances of a practical sort. Sometimes the king laid on too heavily. Sometimes his officers, without his

knowledge and against his desires, acted in an arbitary fashion, extorting extra money from his subjects, imprisoning or fining them in an irregular manner, and otherwise laying exactions, burdens, and inconveniences upon them or depriving them of concrete rights which they had hitherto enjoyed by immemorial custom. Nothing was more natural than that the representatives of the estates, when assembled for purposes of voting taxes, should consider their grievances and come to agreement about them. Hence parliaments soon began to list their protests in the form of petitions to the king for redress. If he approved a petition, it became a law, binding on his officers and subjects. Since the parliament held the purse strings, it could often compel the king to consent, even though it pained him to do so. In due time, the petition was dropped for the bill—a proposed measure drafted in and passed by the parliament. Thus the tax-voting body became a legislature of large powers—everything depending on the character of the monarch and the willfulness of the parliament.

3. The third stage was reached by a gradual process culminating in the revolutions of the seventeenth century. At last, the king was substantially deprived of law-making and tax-voting powers, and his civil and military administration was confined within the limits laid down in constitutional measures. In other words, the estates summoned in the beginning to supply the royal treasury became conscious of their potential powers and transformed themselves into a sovereign body. Their crowning act was to compel the king to choose his chief officers of state, his cabinet or inner council, from the party that had a majority in Parliament. Although an elaborate ideology was developed in the course of this struggle, the operation itself involved a concern with very practical matters, largely economic in character, rather than a moral straining after a general ideal or the best of all possible worlds. When once the ruling classes represented in Parliament gained their ends, they settled down to the enjoyment of the spoils of office in the fashion meticulously described by L. B. Namier in *The Structure of Politics at the Accession of George III*.

4. The economic estates that made themselves sovereign through representative institutions had not long enjoyed the fruits of their labors when rumblings were heard below, among the nameless and unhonored masses that had not shared in the process—serfs who, though rightless in the Middle Ages, had now become freeholders or agricultural laborers, craftsmen in towns, and other

persons from whom the suffrage had been withheld. Indeed, these rumblings had been heard early—in the time of the Peasants' Revolt during the Middle Ages, and especially in the tempestuous age when Cromwell was upsetting the throne. But they were turned into a loud roar by the French Revolution, whose prophet, Rousseau, declared that all men were equal, and that each one was entitled to an equal share in governing. This, of course, was flatly contradictory to the system of English classes, but in time it prevailed—with the gradual extension of the suffrage until in our own time all adult men and women, as such, without regard to property are included within the political pale. And this extraordinary outcome, entirely unforeseen by the founders of representative institutions, was largely the result of a movement of economic, intellectual, and educational forces outside the sphere of legislation and administration.

It was by these stages, speaking cursorily, that we got down to the modern conception of representative government, which may be summarized in the following fashion. Speaking politically, all adult heads are equal and alike, each having an equal share of governing power (whatever that may be). The sovereign power of government is exercised either by constitutional conventions or parliaments composed of deputies elected by the voters. Logically applied, this principle means that the representatives shall be distributed among districts containing substantially the same number of inhabitants, and shall be chosen by majority or plurality vote. Duly assembled, the delegates shall organize themselves and proceed to the exercise of their authority by majority rule. In other words, the political assembly no longer represents estates, classes, or orders as such, but free and equal heads—abstract political persons.

Although there were variations in the theory and many deviations in practice, this conception seemed in a fair way to conquer the world at the opening of the twentieth century. Even China, after living under despotic government for five thousand years, "off and on," as a philosopher once put it, arose from her slumbers and tried the parliamentary experiment—with disastrous results. And during the world conflict that broke out in 1914, the most popular slogan was "Make the world safe for democracy." It is true that President Wilson had said in his *Congressional Government* (p. 227), written in 1888, that "the British government is perfect in proportion as it is unmonarchical, and ours safe in proportion as it is undemocratic;" but that was forgotten during the turmoil of battle. All the world was to go over to representative democracy; and for a time, it seemed almost axiomatic in politics.

Yet long before "the great crusade" began, this Euclidian theory of representative democracy had been vigorously challenged in many quarters. Monarchs and landed aristocracies, real and vestigial, from the Baltic to the Mediterranean, resisted its onward march with all the powers of police and ideology as a matter of course. But there were doubts also in countries that had accepted and applied the doctrine with more or less completeness. Conservatives were disgruntled with representative democracy because it seemed to be growing radical, imposing heavy burdens of taxes on large fortunes, and assuming "improper" functions in the nature of social services. Some of their spokesmen . . . suggested a revision of the canonical creed and the substitution of the representation of economic classes or groups for the representation of free and equal heads. And so zealously did they push their agitation that they produced quite a furor among the theorists, particularly in the academic world.

At the other end of the scale, syndicalists and radical socialists made war on representative democracy. They insisted that heads were not, and could not be, free and equal as long as there were great discrepancies in wealth, that elections and campaigns were farcical since the press and schools were on the side of the heaviest economic battalions, and that the mass of the people suffered from poverty and unemployment under the representative scheme of perfection as under all other systems. The social reforms which conservatives denounced as dangerous, socialists and syndicalists condemned as paltry or insufficient, going on to demand yet more revolutionary installments. Despairing of winning adequate majorities to their cause by the ordinary processes of agitation, they began to demand government by economic parliaments—assemblies composed of members representing the proletariat alone, the proletariat organized at the bottom as workers' councils in factories. After the close of the World War, encouraged by the Soviet experiment in Russia, they renewed their onslaught on representative democracy of the type that had become almost traditional. So at the very moment when this institutional device seemed about to sweep the world, it was rudely challenged; its adequacy for the economic tasks of the technological age was questioned in quarters high and low; and the theory that once looked as sound as the multiplication table was everywhere subjected to critical examination.

From this brief and sweeping survey, certain conclusions seem to emerge. Representative government originated in an agricultural age as an instrument of central authority, dictatorial in substance if monarchical in form, to secure the obedient coöperation of classes as yet only dimly conscious of any urge to the exercise of authority. It spread discipline over these classes, drew them into functions not of their own deliberate designing, gave them knowledge and experience in the field of government, and awakened in them a sense of power. At the same time, amazing instrumentalities for the distribution of political information facilitated the transfer of expertness and comprehension from the monopolists at the center to the very edges of the social periphery. In this way, arbitrary government under royal direction was transformed into parliamentary government resting on a broad popular base. Thus monarchy, which began as a kind of military dictatorship, created for its own uses an agency that ultimately deprived it of sovereignty. Meanwhile, vast masses had become literate and conscious of powers and potentialities. Men who were not by nature political animals were made such by parliamentary discipline. Apparently, by a similar process, illiterate and unconscious masses in other portions of the world may also be transformed into political animals. But, unless there is a general decay of civilization, it is doubtful whether the operation can be reversed, and those once awakened can again be reduced to cogs in an automatic machine deriving its momentum from the center—at all events, for long periods of time as measured by historical standards.

Doubts on this score are accentuated by the course of economic evolution. Since the origin of representative government, the technological revolution has intervened. For various reasons, economic institutions have become highly centralized in the most advanced industrial nations, and governmental activities have multiplied in response to new forces. Conceivably, political functions, confined largely to police and finance, could remain centralized and despotic for a long period in an agricultural society in which economy is localized and self-sufficient, assuming astute management at the center. But when both economy and politics are centralized and cannot proceed effectively without coöperation from top to bottom —wise consideration for popular welfare at the top and loyal coöperation at the bottom—then it becomes doubly doubtful whether it is possible to keep the organism long in motion from heat generated merely at the center. Again we return to a consideration of representative government in evolution as one aspect of the movement of civilization.

Speaking philosophically, the issue before us is not one of attack or defense, but of understanding, as far as our limited intelligence will permit. Speaking practically, the question is one of convenience and utility. Is representative government in any form competent for the tasks of modern society? Is it possible to settle all social conflicts within the limits of law and rationality by discussion and public resolution? Can a great society, confronting difficult technological problems, retain the loyalty of its people without drawing them into intimate coöperative relations with its government and national economy? Can any kind of a dictatorship, no matter how benevolent, deal effectively, in the long run, with collective requirements? And finally, in last analysis, will it be found necessary to make modifications in the structure and operation of representative government with a view to reaching a higher technical proficiency? If so, what is to be the nature of those modifications?

Suggestions for Further Reading

Those who want to pursue further the four models, or styles, of representation presented in this volume—Trustee, Delegate, Partisan, Politico—should be encouraged, initially, to read the larger work, as the case may be, from which the selections herein have been drawn. In almost every case, each contributor's more complex understanding of styles of representation will be found in the larger body of his own writings.

For additional light on the representative as Trustee, however, one can turn to several of Burke's countrymen. Thus Henry Brougham advocates the Trustee role in Volume III of his *Political Philosophy* (London: Bohn, 1849). In Chapter VI he deals with the extension of democracy and the representative principle and defines the concept of political representative. Brougham holds that the representative is chosen by the people to exercise fully and freely for a limited time the power the people gave him to the end that he may perform that aspect of government which the people would otherwise have performed themselves. James Bryce in his *Modern Democracies* (New York: Macmillan, 1921), Chapter LIX, pp. 345–358, reduces the possible roles of the representative to three and himself opts for the role of Trustee. Bryce maintains that the representative should have full freedom upon all questions except those on which he has pledged himself to a definite position. In his classic work, *The American Commonwealth* (New York: Macmillan, 1st American edition, 1889), Bryce in Volume 1, pp. 296–298, maintains that the United States falls short of the four essentials of an excellent representative system. Francis G. Wilson in his work, *The Elements of Modern Politics* (New York: McGraw-Hill, 1936), also advocates the Trustee position as an ideal. In Chapter XIV, "Principles of Representation," he examines several aspects of representative government, and poses the problem of representational roles.

Despite the seemingly idealistic tone of the largely normative defense of the representative as a Trustee, many recent empirically-oriented studies seem to provide support for this role. Thus, observers of the role of Congress in both domestic and foreign policy have noted the relative freedom the representative may have to follow his own ideas without undue worries about an informed, active, and indignant constituency. Thus, Charles O. Jones, in writing on "The Role of the Campaign in Congressional Politics," in Chapter 2 of M. Ken Jennings and L. Harmon Zeigler, editors, *The Electoral Process* (Englewood Cliffs: Prentice-Hall, 1966), notes that the voters "are almost totally unaware of issues in congressional elections and a majority are unaware of the candidates." The campaign period, he writes, "is not an issue-oriented event, and campaign-electoral conditions are such that the representative need not be bound by the election in his policy-making behavior. . . . Furthermore . . . one should not expect the representative to bind himself to electoral returns." A representative's freedom may be even greater in foreign policy. In his study of *Congress and Foreign Policy* (New York: Harcourt, Brace, 1950), Robert A. Dahl noted in Chapter II, "The Congressman and His Public," that on balance, "so far as their constituents are concerned, most Congressmen probably have much more discretion on foreign policy (at least within a very wide range of alternatives) than is often supposed." Dahl concedes that "in the ethos of American democratic politics" the Delegate theory "has probably somewhat wider influence than Burke's own view," yet "it would be wrong to conclude that some such view as Burke's does not persist, particularly as part of the legislator's own idealized conception of himself." See also James A. Robinson, *Congress and Foreign Policy-Making* (Homewood: Dorsey Press, 1962) for interviews of sizable samples of members of Congress by means of structured survey instruments.

The Delegate theory has also had its British and American supporters. Hillaire Belloc and Cecil Chesterson, for example, strongly argued in their book, *The Party System* (London: Swift, Stephen, 1911), that in a democratic system the legislator should vote as his constituents would, if consulted. And Parke Godwin in his *Political Essays* (New York: Dix, Edwards, 1856), vehemently contended in his first chapter that the representative should be a Delegate and should abandon his private selfish interests to perform his duties according to his constituents' wishes. A number of empirical studies suggest that often he does, in fact, function as a Delegate. Thomas A. Flinn and Harold L. Wolman in a recent study, "Constituency and Roll Call Voting: The Case of Southern Democratic Congressmen," *Midwest Journal of Political Science,* Volume X, Number 2 (May, 1966), pp. 192–199, found that of 36 urban and 42 rural Southern

Democratic Congressmen studied there was a definite positive relationship between the representative and his constituency's interests and electoral habits. Wilder Crane also concluded, on the basis of evidence on a daylight saving bill before the Wisconsin Assembly, that a majority of representatives acted as their constituencies' delegates despite their personal judgments. See his article, "Do Representatives Represent?" in the *Journal of Politics*, Volume 22, Number 2 (May, 1960), pp. 295–299. Although the two studies above are somewhat limited, other empirical studies provide additional support for the proposition that the constituency does influence the character and voting of the representative. Thus, Lewis A. Froman, Jr., finds—not surprisingly—that liberals come from "liberal" districts and conservatives from "conservative" districts; and that constituency differences partially explain voting independent of party. In this study he was examining the relationship between the competitiveness of districts, roll-call votes, and constituency factors. See his *Congressmen and Their Constituencies* (Chicago: Rand McNally, 1963), particularly Chapters 7, 8, and 9. In an earlier, pioneering empirical study, Stuart A. Rice investigated two hypotheses: that voters tend to select men of their own kind; and that legislators respond to issues, on the whole, in the same manner as their constituents. See his *Quantitative Methods in Politics* (New York: Knopf, 1928), particularly Chapter 14. See also Duncan MacRae, Jr., "The Relation Between Roll Call Votes and Constituencies in the Massachusetts House of Representatives," in Heinz Eulau, Samuel Eldersveld, and Morris Janowitz, editors, *Political Behavior* (Glencoe: Free Press, 1956), pp. 317–324. MacRae found party irregularity highest in marginal and atypical constituencies, a fact which suggests the significance of such a district on the representative's voting. For a study more difficult for the beginning student see MacRae's *Dimensions of Congressional Voting: A Statistical Study of the House of Representatives* (Berkeley: University of California Press, 1958) in which he attempts to isolate clearly-defined variables by roll-call analysis. William C. Mitchell in an article, "Occupational Role Strains: The American Elective Public Official," discusses seven sources of strain and concludes that it is impossible for any politician to ignore public opinion. See the *Administrative Science Quarterly*, Volume 3, Number 1 (September, 1958), pp. 210–228.

For general arguments on the importance of role of the responsible Partisan see E. E. Schattschneider, *Party Government* (Farrar & Rinehart, 1942), *The Struggle for Party Government* (College Park,

Md.: University of Maryland Press, 1948), *The Semisovereign People* (New York: Holt, Rinehart and Winston, 1960), Austin Ranney, *The Doctrine of Responsible Party Government* (Urbana: University of Illinois Press, 1962), James MacGregor Burns, *The Deadlock of Democracy* (Englewood Cliffs: Prentice-Hall, 1963). The student will also want to consult the congressional hearings in 1945, and again in 1965, on the subject of the organization and reform of Congress, and for specific testimony on behalf of more responsible party membership. Malcolm E. Jewell notes the importance of parties in his study of "Party Voting in American State Legislatures," *American Political Science Review,* Volume XLIX, Number 3 (September, 1955), pp. 773–791. Jewell, using the roll-call method of analysis, examines party cohesiveness in eight state legislatures. However, William Keefe raises doubts about the significance of partisanship in state legislatures. See his "Parties, Partisanship, and Public Policy in the Pennsylvania Legislature," *American Political Science Review,* Volume XLVIII, Number 2 (June, 1954), pp. 450–464; and his "Comparative Study of the Role of Political Parties in State Legislatures," *Western Political Quarterly,* Volume IX, (September, 1956). For the empirical controversy on the method of roll-call analysis in determining the effect of party influence and party loyalty, see Wilder Crane's questions on this method in "A Caveat on Roll-Call Studies of Party Voting," *Midwest Journal of Political Science,* Volume IV, Number 3 (August, 1960), pp. 237–249; and a rejoinder by Fred I. Greenstein and Alton F. Jackson, "A Second Look at the Validity of Roll Call Analysis," *Midwest Journal of Political Science,* Volume VII (May, 1963), pp. 156–166. It might also be noted here that Julius Turner, despite the fact that he is grouped with advocates of more responsible partisanship in this volume, did not necessarily agree with their policy recommendations. Indeed, his "Responsible Parties: A Dissent from the Floor," *The American Political Science Review,* Volume XLV (March, 1951), pp. 143–152, is required reading for uncritical admirers of the report of the Committee on Political Parties of the American Political Science Association. Turner argues that the committee underestimates present party responsibility; he maintains that party alternatives are distinguishable and that most of the majority program is carried out, and that some committee reforms might accentuate present defects in our party system.

For an earlier argument on behalf of the representative as a Politico see Arnold Bennett Hall, *Popular Government* (New York: Macmillan, 1921), particularly Chapter III, "Representative Government and Direct Democracy." Hall conceives the ideal representative as a Politico who fulfills his personal and party pledges, adheres to the key decisions of the party caucus, votes in accordance with a real public opinion if it exists, but who decides according to personal conviction in the absence of a true and known public opinion. Warren E. Miller and Donald E. Stokes conclude, too, in their more empirical study of "Constituency Influence in Congress" that the American representative is a Politico who assumes a different representative role in moving from one policy domain to another. In this study they analyze the representative-constituency relationship for 116 congressmen, their opponents, and their constituents, on such issues as social and economic welfare, foreign affairs, and civil rights. They find, by the way, a great deal of constituent unawareness regarding their congressmen. Austin Ranney in *The Governing of Men* (New York: Holt, Rinehart and Winston (Revised edition, 1966), also concludes that the American representative is a Politico. See particularly Chapters 12 and 17 where Ranney examines the general nature of political representation, representational problems, and the classic argument between Delegate and Trustee. He also contrasts British and American representatives in their relations with their constituents.

Other models of the role of the representative may be examined and contrasted to the four presented herein. For example, a very astute observer, Lewis Anthony Dexter, calls our attention to what we might call a "transactional" model in his chapter, "The Job of the Congressman," in Raymond A. Bauer, Ithiel de Sola Pool, and Lewis Anthony Dexter, *American Business and Public Policy: The Politics of Foreign Trade* (New York: Atherton Press, 1963). Dexter emphasizes in Chapters 29 and 30 the congressman's great freedom to define his own role: to decide selectively what decisions to consider: how to use his time, allocate his resources, mobilize his energy, listen or not, respond or not, to constituents, interest groups, party, colleagues, and other pressures. For his earlier statement of this theme, see his "The Representative and His District," *Human Organization,* Volume 16, Number 1 (Spring, 1957), pp. 2–13. For another model see Roger H. Davidson, David M. Kovenock, and Michael K. O'Leary, *Congress in Crisis: Politics and Congressional Reform* (Belmont, Calif.: Wadsworth Publishing Company, 1966), pp. 73–75, "Congressmen Define Their Roles." They interpret role in terms of the congressman's purpose or his interpretation of the "ultimate aims of his activities" and come up with five roles:

"Tribune" (determining, representing, and protecting the interests of the people), "Ritualist" (debating, voting, attending to hearings, investigations, and other committee work), "Inventor," (problem solving), "Broker" (weighing and balancing competing interests), and "Opportunist" (campaigning and gaining reelection). The first two ranked highest in the eyes of the 87 members of the 88th Congress (1963–64) examined. For the full-scale Wahlke-Eulau-Buchanan-Ferguson model, see their *The Legislative System* (New York: Wiley, 1962), p. 14. For a most comprehensive composite model, see Malcolm E. Jewell and Samuel C. Patterson, *The Legislative Process in the United States* (New York: Random House, 1966), p. 384. This book also provides an excellent summary of the literature and findings in the field.

For an excellent comparative round-up of the literature see Wilder W. Crane, Jr., Chapter 15, "Legislators and the Formulation of Public Policy," in Alex N. Dragnich, John C. Wahlke et al, *Government and Politics* (New York: Random House, 1966), pp. 483–489. Crane analyzes the social and economic backgrounds of American and European legislators, the Wahlke-Eulau study of the role of the representative, informal legislative norms, and the findings of roll-call studies. Other broad-gaged comparative studies are Carl J. Friedrich, *Constitutional Government and Democracy* (Boston: Little, Brown, 1941). This edition throws valuable historical and analytical light on such topics as "General Problems of Representation" (Chapter 14), "Parliaments as Representative Assemblies" (Chapter 20), and "Direct Popular Action" (Chapter 24). See also Friedrich's *Man and His Government: An Empirical Theory of Politics* (New York: McGraw-Hill, 1963), Chapter 17, "Political Representation and Responsibility." Other comparative studies include Herman Finer's *Theory and Practice of Modern Government* (New York: Holt, revised edition, 1949), particularly pp. 219 ff and pp. 369–377 for treatment of problems most important in the study of representative government; Gabriel A. Almond and James S. Coleman, editors, *The Politics of the Developing Areas* (Princeton: Princeton University Press, 1960); and Elke Frank, editor, *Lawmakers in a Changing World* (Englewood Cliffs; Prentice-Hall, 1966).

Among other general works one should also consult Harold F. Gosnell's *Democracy: The Threshold of Freedom* (New York: Ronald, 1948), particularly the second part. This is a first-rate study of the nature of representation and of the evolution and operation of representative government. Gosnell critically examines the relation of the legislator to his constituents, what the voter should expect of his representative, how the legislator responds to political pressures, how voters may exercise control over legislators, and the tools the voter has to perform the tasks of democracy. For a review of views on "The Nature of Political Representative," see John A. Fairlie's article on that theme in *The American Political Science Review*, Volume XXXIV (April and June, 1940), starting at pp. 236 and 456 respectively. Fairlie explores the origin, development and characteristics of representative government. One should not neglect the light that *The Federalist* throws on the question of representation and the role of the representative. Madison, in Number 10 *Federalist*, viewed representation as a refinement of the popular will and as a cure for the evils of faction. John Stuart Mill in his classic essay, *Representative Government*, argues for representative government as ideally best, but he does not probe styles of representation. "The Fascist Concept of Representation," is explored by Rene de Visme Williamson with great insight in *The Journal of Politics*, Volume III, Number 1 (February, 1941), pp. 29–41. Those who are interested in earlier patterns of representation might explore them in J.A.O. Larsen's *Representative Government in Greek and Roman History* (Berkeley: University of California Press, 1966). For a general round-up on research the student may conveniently refer to bibliographical articles by Norman Meller: "Legislative Behavior Research," and "Legislative Behavior Research Revisited," *Western Political Quarterly*, Volume 13, Number 1 (March, 1960), pp. 131–153, and Volume 18, Number 4 (December, 1965), pp. 776–793. The first article summarizes the literature and notes that relatively little has been done in the area of legislative roles. The second article claims that recent research has distinguished itself by its rigorous theory, inventive empiricism, and broad inquiry.

The student may also profitably consult some of the more general books on Congress which help to illuminate the broader context of styles of representation. A few of these may suffice: Bertram Gross, *The Legislative Struggle* (New York: McGraw-Hill, 1953); Donald R. Matthews, *U.S. Senators and Their World* (Chapel Hill: University of North Carolina Press, 1960); David B. Truman, editor, *The Congress and America's Future* (Englewood Cliffs: Prentice-Hall, 1965); John F. Bibby and Roger H. Davidson, *On Capital Hill: Studies in the Legislative Process* (New York: Holt, Rinehart, and Winston, 1966). The Bibby-Davidson book is a description and analysis of various phases of congressional life: e.g., campaigns, the congressional routine, party organization and functioning, the committee system, the impact of the rules, relation to the President as legislator. Finally, for a realistic account of *The Congressman: His Work as He Sees It,* one may consult Charles L. Clapp's book by that title (Washington: The Brookings Institute, 1963), and the revealing letters of Clem Miller, *Member of the House: Letters of a Congressman* (New York: Charles Scribner's Sons, 1962).

4-300